Given to Praise!

Given to Praise!

*An array of provocative
metaphysical — philosophical
utterances*

by Kenneth G. Mills

*edited with preface and notes
by* Jaan Koel

Sun-Scape Publications
Toronto

This book is dedicated

to all books of meaning

which are caught

in the twilight zone

and wait to be freed

out of the reading habit

and into a way of life.

The first edition published by Sun-Scape Publications
Ltd., c/o 349 Berkeley Street, Toronto, Ontario, Canada
M5A 2X6
ISBN 0-919842-00-3

This book is also available in record form under the
same title and read by the author for your sound
pleasure. Enquiries may be directed to the
publisher.

Printed in Canada

Highlights

Acknowledgements

In the joy of having found one in the name of Jaan Koel to place the statements in this book into a framework of flowing lines (a wave unto your edge of perception), gratitude is expressed by the giver of the Unfoldments. In this stream of acknowledging, thanks and appreciation ride the wave to all those heard and unheard who have played parts in this composition. The act of bowing to the Unseen is ever the natural key to unlocking any word of meaning when it has been given as an act of Love. Included in this acknowledgement are Priscilla Costello and Teresa Stevens for typing the many drafts of the manuscript, and for their constructive comments. Special thanks go to Dr. Pier Paolo Alberghini, Jurij Bochna and Gerald Johnson for the photographs, and to Richard Leach for the drawings. Appreciation is extended to Ian Jaffray for contributing his time in doing the paste-up work for this book, and to Ian Tudhope and Beverly Tudhope for their viable suggestions pertaining to the design.

Kenneth G. Mills

Kenneth G. Mills lives in Toronto, Ontario, Canada. He was born in the Maritimes, in St. Stephen, New Brunswick, where he lived for the first seventeen years of his life. His early years were frequented by experiences in precognition and astral travel, which, in spite of their challenging nature at the time, sparked an interest later in his life in exploring the mysteries of higher levels of consciousness. Mr. Mills developed a great affinity for music during these years, and chose the piano as his focus. He progressed exceptionally well and by the time he was fifteen years old knew that music was to be his career. Mr. Mills moved to Toronto in the early 1940's on a private scholarship, and this marked the beginning of an intensive nine year period of preparation in order to become a concert pianist.

His ambition was finally realized in 1952 when Mr. Mills made his formal Canadian debut in Toronto. The performance was very successful and established him as one of the fine performers on his instrument in Canada. Shortly after his debut, Mr. Mills married, his wife also being a musician and music teacher. The marriage lasted for ten years, at which point they mutually agreed to separate so that each could fulfill his destiny in his own way.

After parting from his wife, Mr. Mills began a very quiet, contemplative life in a small house in north Toronto, where he continued practising and teaching piano to a group of selected students. Mr. Mills continued to concertize and in 1962 made his American debut at Town Hall in New York City. Yet, in spite of his increasing reputation as a fine pianist, the glamour and

9

attraction of concertizing was fading. In the seclusion of his new environment, he began pursuing his life-long interest in and affinity for the Divine with more intensity than ever before. His life was changing. Mr. Mills started to use the incredible mental tool that he had developed through his rugged discipline in music towards a deeper, more significant purpose. He turned the bright light of his honed mentality towards the Self, towards God-Realization.

In 1965 Mr. Mills was asked to do a world tour which would last for one year. On the morning of the day on which he was to sign the contract with the impressario, who was then returning to Europe, Mr. Mills was intuitively guided to decline the offer, to turn down the opportunity that he had waited for and dreamed of all his life. Needless to say, the impressario, along with Mr. Mills' family and friends, was stunned. This is what he had been working towards for twenty-five years! Nevertheless, Mr. Mills stood firm on his intuition, sensing that a tremendous change in his life was now imminent.

This change began to manifest itself in a matter of weeks. One evening Mr. Mills received a very unusual telephone call from a friend who had just had a consultation with a psychic medium. Upon asking the medium what her purpose in Mr. Mills' life was, she had received the reply, "You are to tell Mr. Mills that he must learn to speak the word again." Mr. Mills was puzzled by this message, especially since he had never considered himself a speaker. Nonetheless, he was open to the message and knew that it would clarify itself as long as he didn't get in the way by trying to interpret it.

A short while later, Mr. Mills went out with a friend to hear a visiting Buddhist monk who was giving a series of three lectures in Toronto. The monk was en route to his home in Thailand and spoke haltingly to his English-speaking audience. Several times during the series when the monk was about to use the incorrect English word or phrase, he caught the eye of Mr. Mills, who would shake his head and the monk would pause, close his eyes, and then somehow come up with the correct English word. When the last lecture was over, and after most of the people had left the hall, Mr. Mills' friend, having sensed the extraordinary communication that had occurred between the monk and Mr. Mills, whispered, "Are you not going to go up and speak with him?" Mr. Mills replied, "No, I've already talked to him with my eyes." No sooner had he said this than the Buddhist announced in a booming, decisive tone that no one had yet heard, "Words are important. You must learn to speak the word again!" Mr. Mills was astonished. He approached the monk and spoke with him for a moment saying that he felt he had spoken to him with his eyes. The monk repeated, "Yes, yes, but words are important; you must learn to speak the word again!"

Mr. Mills now knew that this message was of paramount importance in his life, even though he did not fully understand what it meant. In the days that followed, Mr. Mills inwardly renounced all his ideas on what he thought his life was and where he thought it was going. He realized more clearly than ever that the Will of God was written in his heart, and agreed to do whatever it was that he came to do, especially to speak if he were asked to do so. Since that day Mr. Mills' speaking has been a miracle. His discourses are given directly and spontaneously, in prose and poetry, from the Source, from Consciousness itself. His many years of inner searching and enquiry, as well as the mental discipline afforded him by his piano studies, have all culminated in the unique way in which he is able to pour forth in words the riches of the high state of Self-Consciousness.

From a handful of listeners in 1967, the number of those who have come to meet with Mr. Mills and hear his moving verbal meditations has grown steadily. Up until the spring of 1975 Mr. Mills was still actively involved musically as a highly respected piano teacher and adjudicator. At that time, however, the increasing demands made upon him by those interested in hearing him required that he discontinue his teaching and adjudicating. Today he is a man of fifty-three totally engaged in the work of the Self, which of course encompasses the lives of all his students. Aside from his weekly talks, or *Unfoldments* as they are called, which are given at his home and at various universities and auditoriums in Toronto, Mr. Mills has also been conducting intensive and exciting workshops in Canada, Italy, and the United States. A new American Centre for the Unfoldments has recently been established near Tucson, Arizona.

Over the years, Mr. Mills has influenced people from virtually every walk of life. The people that hear him today are dedicated to living the Principle that he so beautifully voices and evidences. The Unfoldments are complete in their efficacy in that they not only point to the freedom inherent within the inner world of the individual, but also underline the corresponding freedom, order, and success so essential to the outer world of action and professional accomplishment.

If you are interested in becoming acquainted with Mr. Mills and attending his Unfoldments, workshops, or the Summer Festival of Light, Peace, and Sound, which is held each year during July and August in Muskoka, Ontario, you are welcome to write to him in care of the publisher.

Preface

This book is a collage of aphorisms, poems, and excerpts from the Unfoldments that have been spoken by Mr. Kenneth G. Mills. They have been selected from a vast library of recorded conversations that he has had with numerous people during the past eight years. In response to the many requests made to Mr. Mills by his students and friends to have his meditations in print comes the first formal publication of his words, *Given to Praise!* Before proceeding with the preface, I wish to state that it has been an honour to be the one to whom was given the privilege of editing and preparing this book, of putting onto paper a representation of this man's life, his raison d'être. Having known Mr. Mills for the past seven years, and having lived in his household and been in his employ for three, has been the inspiration and impetus to an inner journey in awareness that I never dreamt possible. The many valuable hours spent with Mr. Mills going over the manuscript, changing, shaping, moulding, discovering, have not only resulted in the refinement of a book, but of myself as well, and for this I am eternally grateful to him, my Teacher.

What is it that Mr. Mills speaks about? He speaks of that Universal Somethingness that is common to us all: Consciousness. What is Consciousness? That is a question that has never been fully answered. Consciousness as it IS cannot be totally defined in terms of thought, simply because it is beyond thought, beyond the mental descriptions and images of the mind. Consciousness is and can only be known, and when once realized in and as experience, can be effectively pointed to via appropriate words and actions. To Mr. Mills, Consciousness is no question, yet as he has said, all questions are evidence of it and point to it. Consciousness is the only experience there is, says Mr. Mills, and whatever we are able to discern about the world, ourselves and others are all *events* of Consciousness. There is only One such Consciousness, and this One Consciousness is what we all in Essence are.

To hear Kenneth Mills speak is an exciting experience. His totally extemporaneous talks are called "Unfoldments" — an apt title for the ever-blossoming, spontaneous expression of Conscious Realization that he evidences. The Unfoldments are fresh, alive, and penetrating, and are given by Mr. Mills in both prose and poetry. They are like a river: the water is always water, but the variety and delight of the form is endless. His words, gestures, and actions flow together and often possess a magical humour — and they also express the penetrating authority that comes from a deepened understanding. Whatever form his expression may take, Mr. Mills always points to what the experience of life can be when lived in the radical understanding of what Life IS.

What Life IS is the whole point of the Unfoldments. To Mr. Mills, Life in its true sense means to live wholly in the awareness and from the standpoint of One, as opposed to the chaos of duality or separateness. In spite of their True Nature, men and women continually fall for the dualistic products of their minds. The mind or thought faculty operates to conceptualize and compartmentalize experience into a subject-object framework, the framework of duality or relativity where there is the perceiver and the thing perceived — the thinker and his thoughts. Mr. Mills has often stated that the mind functions like a prism in that it diffuses the pure Light of Consciousness, which is One, into the spectrum of concepts which we call our life experience. Today's man falls for this natural process of the mind and believes its products to be reality. He has created a reality out of the intellectual concepts that he has manufactured and used to merely symbolize his experiences in Consciousness, which in essence and by nature are non-rational, that is to say "beyond the mind," to quote Mr. Mills. The most powerful of these concepts are "self," "world," and "other," and under these three categories fall all the other concepts and symbols of experience. In his Unfoldments Mr. Mills questions the validity of these concepts as things in themselves, which they have largely

become, and points in his inimitable way to the fact that these concepts are not reality, but that Consciousness IS, and is the Light to
all symbolic creations of the mind. This idea is present in the
following statement of Mr. Mills':

It's your awareness
that motivates your actions;
it's your intellect that limits them.

What of a rose? Can it be "understood"? Can
anyone compose a formula for the beauty and fragrance there? The
concept "rose" is describable in terms of other concepts, but its
actual experience (which we refer to as "perception") is not. No
matter the number of petals, anthers or stamens that are supposed
to comprise this extraordinary occurrence, the rose will always
remain what it is: an event of Consciousness.

This leads us to consider the topic of imagination,
which is of great significance in Mr. Mills' work. He has said that it
is the unbridled or untrained imagination that has created in our
minds the notion of a limited objective reality, a world of separate
things of which we are part, and to which we fall victim. By
magnifying and distorting the collective input of dualistic concepts,
which have comprised the bulk of our education, the unchecked
imagination has created the illusion of duality and objectivity out
of what was and what always is in Essence a unified World of
Consciousness.

The imaging faculty, however, is capable of being
trained, "redeemed" as the author says, to structure the life experience not upon notions, but upon the Principle that Consciousness is
the basis of existence. The imagination structures and responds to
the entire gamut of conceptual images and symbols that we call our
world and our life. Not to allow these mental images or symbols to
become objectified into the false notion of an "outside" world, a
reality separate and apart from Consciousness, is the task of the
disciplined, "redeemed" imagination. When this is practised in daily
life, the symbols and concepts which we deal with are still there,
but we are able to see through them; we are able to see "through

the looking glass" of mirrored concepts and fall not for their reflection as the total experience. The following given by Mr. Mills states this very point:

> **The redeemed imagination enables you**
> **to see the picture through the looking glass**
> **and appear to be in that land**
> **but filled with the wonder**
> **at the miracle of clear sight.**

Certainly concepts and thoughts constitute a most salient aspect of our daily lives. We use them all the time to construct a common platform and reference for communication. The basic vehicle that we use for communicating — in fact, what communication itself consists of — is thought. Yet this tool of ours has to be viewed and used very carefully as is stressed in the following statement by Mr. Mills:

> **One thought**
> **thought to be yours**
> **is the wall between Heaven**
> **and earth.**

That which is "yours", that which is closest to you, which in fact is what you are, is Consciousness (Heaven). A thought "thought to be yours" (earth) refers to a thought or a notion, or to all thoughts and notions collectively which have been mistakenly believed to be Consciousness, or true Experience. Thought can only be an echo of Conscious Experience. It is a description; it is not the Source. Yet, paradoxically, it is not separate from the Source either. There is really no wall. Consider the following statement:

> **The Source is the Substance**
> **to any thought about it.**

Here Mr. Mills states that the countless thoughts that arise do so from within the same Substance; they arise as ever-changing, kaleidoscopic forms lighted by Consciousness. Our

16

mental habit is one that continually mistakes the myriad changing forms to be Reality, rather than Consciousness which is what lights up the entire changing picture of man and his world. A life lived in Conscious Realization is one freed from conceptual limits, one that is lived in understanding and the active application of this understanding moment to moment. A Realized Life is enjoyed in a complete and harmonious relationship with the world and others because it is perceived that the world and others are arising within Consciousness.

An all-too-familiar trend of the mind is that it will discard a precious jewel because of its inability to understand and therefore recognize it. The mighty emphasis that we have placed upon intellectual understanding has unfortunately reduced our capacity to intuitively perceive and appreciate what is not rational, what is non-conceptual, what is "beyond the mind." All too frequently do we accept something only when it makes "sense" to us and fills our biased prescriptions for life.

The symbols that Mr. Mills uses in his Unfoldments can be interpreted on several different levels. As a rule, however, the symbology and meaning is to be taken primarily on a metaphysical level. It is on this level that direct reference is made to the many aspects and faculties of the reader's mind. Here the Unfoldment is not only a spontaneous work of art, but a practical tool with which to see ourselves more and more clearly. The multivarious attitudes, conscious processes, motives and beliefs that we are constantly acting out are suddenly seen and exposed to the Light of a Principle that is fixed and unchanging. According to this Principle we can either redeem or drop any of the undesirable or limiting elements of the mind that may inhibit conscious unfoldment.

As an example, the symbol "bird" that appears throughout Mr. Mills' book refers to the inspired thought, one which is freed from the mundane. It refers to the state of mind which is able to "fly" above and beyond the earth (i.e. beliefs of matter or suggested objectivity) and into the realms of non-rational, unfiltered experience.

Mr. Mills uses the words "you", "me", "I", and "I AM" in a very specific sense. The *you* and *me*, especially when stressed, refer to the imaginary entities that we have created in our minds and claimed to be the identity of both ourselves and others. The *you* and the *me* represents the state of thought that believes itself to be embodied physically and thus part and parcel of a material world. It is our conceptual identity; it is a limited corporeal self-image that we have been educated to construct on the premise of duality and materiality. In short, it is the human personality that parades one way one minute, and another way the next.

The I AM is the Infinite, the Eternal and the Unchanging. The I or the I AM is our true Identity. The I AM is what we really are. It is beyond any thought that can be identified with the finite. It is not a conceptual identity for it cannot be conceived, yet it is the Light to all conception. The I AM is synonymous with other terms appearing in the text: Consciousness, the Source, the Self, Christ, Truth, Life, Love, the Light, That Which IS. Yet, we cannot think in terms of being That personally, because that would impose a limit on the I AM which is limitless. Mr. Mills gives this very clearly in the following statements:

> **I points to Being.**
> **You call it "you" or "me"**
> **when you think in terms.**
>
> **The I AM**
> **permits man to assume**
> **an "I am" identity;**
> **but the I AM**
> **isn't in the identity.**

Lastly, consider the power of sound. Where does it arise? Who listens? These are the questions that the listener is led to consider when hearing Mr. Mills speak. In music, who could experience its true essence by just reading the score? In the Unfoldments it is being in Mr. Mills' presence and hearing his voice that bears the power to move, and to transform. This book is the "musical score" of numerous spontaneous improvisations and as such can only point to the magnitude of the experience of hearing Mr. Mills. The Unfoldments are magnificent symphonies of sound and can inaugurate tremendous leaps in awareness when one is able to hear and see beyond the symbols called words. What is the experience "rose" beyond the symbol or image of it?

Read, and while reading, listen. Drop the "reading habit" of conceptualizing and categorizing, and hear what Mr. Mills is saying within these pages. Discover for yourself the ever-unfolding "way of life" that Mr. Mills declares in the dedication. To hear the voice of the Free Spirit in man, the voice of his Essence, is to realize that it has always been sounding, both within our hearts and within our world. Wherever and whenever this authentic Tone appears on earth, it soars above the clamour of our own limited thoughts and leads us to Awakening. We must make every effort to listen when such a voice is with us. Such a voice is that of Kenneth G. Mills.

Jaan Koel
Toronto, 1976

Given to Praise!

Event One

*When a book
is opened,
an unseen promise
dwells.*

Thine I Be Single

The setting has already taken place at the right hand of the Father, and the whole picture, be it of the world or the universe, is lighted by the light of understanding, revelation, intuitive awareness, and insight. All these different levels of consciousness are there, and the One Consciousness includes all of them. It only appears in the educational process that you can separate them and say that one is this consciousness and one is that consciousness. It's only a "suffering it to be so now" until the comprehension dawns that the One Consciousness reigns supreme, and in Its supremacy lies man and his universe.

The universe is considered to be the totality of parts, but the universe, in the root system, means to "turn into one."[1] If the thoughts of multiplicity can be swallowed up in the Divinity of One Altogether, then see if there are parts or if they can only appear so that the dance of time may be staged and the choreography so sustained that all who witness the programme may be swallowed up in the effulgence of an act freed from the suggestion of personal dancers and personal gravity surrounding their field of levitation.

It is seen in the dance how men and women defy being grounded and spend hours before the bar in order to leap over the suggestion that there is one present. Yet, in the mirrored reflection, the forms can be seen, becoming or unbecoming to one who would be one with the rhythm and the flow of the musical experience.

24

There's no division; there is only the One.
Regardless of a thousand men, there's only One Man. The one who
does not realize this is one in a mass, and one in a mass is always
in a mess! That's why you stand apart, because you innately know
that the Father of you is the God of you, and that which recognizes
this is Christ Consciousness.

You
is the suggestion
of a creation apart from God.[2]

The greatest belief
to drop
is the belief called *you.*

You are thinking of Oneness
as something that is going to happen;
but it's because it has already happened
and IS
that you are here.
You are projecting it in a time sequence;
but there is only One Event
and that is Now.
There will never be more Allness than
there is right at this moment.

Two is only **One** misconceived.

The difference between your mind and my mind is the suggestion that Consciousness could be divided. Man has had the belief resident within his consciousness that he is a consciousness separate from another consciousness. **There is only One Consciousness**, which is incapable of divisibility. The grace of That which IS enables man to appear to be what he isn't (seemingly divided) until he realizes what he truly IS in the image and likeness of the Son.

> A group is
> the suggestion
> that there is more than
> One gathered together
> in *My* name.

The mental structure that man has created has been based on limitation. He has never conceived of his completeness, of the Infinite Light of Being Altogether One. If I kick you, you'd swear there were two. But if I kick you and you say "Ouch," it's obvious that the consciousness that did it and the one that said "Ouch" is the One that was totally present for the happening. There were not two; it was only belief that created the kicker and the kicked!

A bar in music
was never meant to stop its flow.
It was only there to keep your eyes
on the page
until it was a spontaneous expression,
and you, the participant,
a conscious experience,
One
with the Source of its so-called existence
as it IS,
and not as you think it is.

The purpose of music is to reveal to man his innate
at-Onement with a harmonic state of Being.

Query:
What would be the relationship between the piano and the
music?

Answer:
None. Piano appears to music as person appears to
consciousness. Divide them if you can!

Let us sit and listen, *one as another*.

Man believes and structures his consciousness in such a way that he divides That which has never been divided because he doesn't want to live, move, and do as a wholeness. He wants to do as a fragment, claiming a Wholeness from a fragmentary position. Consciousness appears to be divided because men have been taught what they are not instead of what they are.

When the gate opens,
there is no need for it
as there are no walls.

Time would have you wasted
and space would claim your grave.
When you know that a leaf or a flower
blossomed,
and bowed its head to the wind,
you know that the Unseen Power is present
if you let it in.
Inhale,
and exchange the limited thought
for the idea of All-inclusiveness!

A day
is only the misrepresentation of Eternity.

Silence has nothing to do with noise,
just as Eternity
has nothing to do with time.

The belief of time is the measured lack
of stillness.

A moment
minus
identity — limit
is
Eternity
limited is given identity
and called
a moment.[3]

I is not figured at all in time.

You have no other purpose,
when you cease to think,
than to be what's left over
when thought is done.

Thinking and time are one.
It doesn't take time to think;
so if you don't think,
isn't it marvellous to be Eternal?

A mind
that is stilled
is still the mind.

A minute
is the time given
for man
to sense a thought.

A moment
is the suggestion
that Light could be timed.[4]

Every moment lived in awareness
finds Eternality experienced
as a living Reality.

I points to Being.
You call it *you* or *me*
when you think in terms.[5]

Awareness limited
is sometimes called *me* and *you*.
Awareness unlimited
rejoices as Self-identity.

The aphorisms given are like point upon point which, when traced, can reveal a line. A traced line is sometimes figured; so a line that is traced and recognized is a figure known, and a known figure is often called an embellishment upon a melodic note of prominence in the fulfillment of a theme of pithy significance.

One of the greatest threads in the garment of Self-discovery is the ability to listen so attentively that only I AM heard, and then you may say something that frees one caught in the time-tunnel.[6]

Query:
Mr. Mills, what is it that we should listen for?

Answer:
What *isn't* said.

The seasons roll and turn
and man says man ages.
It isn't man that ages;
it's the belief that ages.
It isn't man that learns to love;
it's a belief that tries to!
When a man appears on the scene
who innately knows *I* love you,
it's not a belief.
A belief takes time to love
because it takes a believer
to believe in love;
but to Love there is no belief
of a believer,
and therefore no time.

Query:
What does it mean to look within?

Answer:
To look within means only to associate with those thoughts that cannot be objectified.[7]

> Miracle
> is the lessening
> of the objective
> confinement.

> The thought world
> is Conscious Experience
> thought to be objective.

Query:
Is thought an experience beyond the thinker?

Answer:
Thought is objectification. As soon as you think about an experience you have objectified it.

Query:
Does the *you* come in when you name the experience?

Answer:
When you believed that the experience stopped, you became an experienc*er*. An experience named wears the garment called *you*.

Experience
is the name of a garment
that a differentiated consciousness wears
until differentiation fades out
and I is All.[8]

If you can experience
Me as I Am,
who is there to testify?
Experience is division;
division is experience.
If no division — no experience — no limit.
I AM ALL.

Query:
Is the Formless formed in experience?

Answer:
Yes. Hi! Why don't you say hello to your Self?

See within, and you will find
where all the objects are truly found —
within mind.

The form is the death of an idea
when considered objectified.

Appearance
is the suggested objectification
of a thought held by one who sleeps.

You
is the result
of language objectified.

Query:
You as the Self are aware of all things?

Answer:
You as the Self are the awareness to the suggestion of all things.

If you are thinking in terms of helping other people, you are thinking in terms, and there are no terms to God-Being.[9]

Freedom is found as
I Am not thought.

Look
is the experience of the subject.

To vision is the looker present?
Or are you hooked by having a vision?

When God and man see
face to face,
who is *there* .. to witness?[10]

Event Two

The body of the Sun
is never seen.
It is only known.

Solar Orb

The Soul structure has to be created.[1]
If you are considering a structure
Found in the drawing room,
Bearing the blueprints pointing to Soul's accomplishment,
Know that it is only a plan,
An ideal,
Whereby you can find yourselves structuring a life that is not
                    limited
To one place,
But a Life that is known to be sponsored
In the Light of Will
And universal
In its adaptations and bestowals.

The sun in your sky
Has been declared to have a body and a gown
Of flames and light.
You say, "If there is no moon, no reflective surface,
There is no proof that the sun is still shining."
And yet just look at your nature
And see;
There is the evidence of its might.
In the action of its impersonal service
The Sun shines
Whether or not you ask it to,
Will it to,
Or sweat because it does!

The great solar orb
Holds your attention

Until you find the Jewel within yourself. The sunflower always
          faces the sun,
And the sunflower bears its heart
Of earth
And its gown of illumination in yellow,
Which is likened unto an intellect being prepared to witness its own
          limitation.[2]
Know that in the limited framework
The Limitless may be experienced
When freed
From the suggestion of "earthling."
You are not an earthling by accident;
You err in considering yourself
To be of earth. Your vehicle of cognition
Cannot be found via earth;
The light of cognition cannot be verified by earth.[3]
But the earth's apparent constancy
Points to a verifiable Point
When you can square all your deals and find the Centre,
And no limit
To the radius of accomplishment.

When you know where the Centre is,
Your radius is limitless. You see,
Limited thought gives limited earthlings
A chance to be at home with nature.
Unfettered thought enables the appearance of earthlings
To be clad
In the freshness of a natural experience,
Yet unlimited to an earth-bound condition.
In the simplicity and the natural experience,
Thought is utilized
As is light.

This system,
That is considered solar,
Is considered because the sun is known to hold the power unto its
          earthlings
And their field of action.
It only took time for the earthling to realize

That when the sun disappeared, it wasn't because it needed a rest,
But because the earth
Couldn't stand
The constant brilliance of its Allness.

The Day is the irradiance of the Sun.
Yet, it was divided into acts: night, sunrise, day, sunset.
Night, sunrise, day, sunset.
Night and day,
I AM the One.
You experience night and day;
I experience only my own Allness,
And declare That from the Mount of Illumination as
I AM That.
I AM That Constant.
I AM Constant I AM.
I AM Light I AM.

Now,
If you can shake the hell
Out of life,
It's obvious that life has only been thought
To be what it isn't.
And the thought presenting life
To be what it isn't
Is the hell that you make out of falling
For a suggestion
That Life could be other than what it IS.
It has nothing whatsoever to do
With what you think it is.
You know not the Light,
Yet you know that in the Light
You see Life an action,
The sun flame
And heat,
Never sleeping,
Never slumbering,
Light always..
Present.

When I looked at a form
I thought I saw . .
that's when time came for you.
When I saw the Formless, time faded;
when I saw my **I**,
Eternity dawned.

When I looked at the Sea,
there was no face around.
How could a time be found?[4]

All is seen, stands revealed.
Sun is risen — earth stands *still*.

Individuality

Query:
Is it not individuality that makes us seem apparently separate from one another?

Answer:
It is the suggestion of individuality that makes you appear separate from one another.

Query:
Then once this state of Oneness is reached, does that separateness also fall away?

Answer:
When you declare your I, how many are there?

Query:
There's only one.

Answer:
It's only when you think that there are two.

Query:
Then in reality we are the same being.

Answer:
In Reality there is no one to declare that we are the same. There is only the rejoicing of the Sameness as Suchness.

Don't ever be afraid of becoming a drop in the ocean, for if you are fed up with your being, and think of yourself as a drip, know that right behind that statement stands That Ocean that enables life as you think it is to be dropped, and Truth as it IS to be embraced.

**The Ideal
is a Conscious State
without ripple or rent.**[5]

This is not the practice of changing beliefs. This is only the practice of disciplining the thought to weave a garment commensurate to the Body that is considered the Ideal Figure. Don't try to change your beliefs; just try to find if there is one!

An Ideal is that which is known — a result of a Principle practised with Love, devotion, sincerity and honesty.

That for which you search cannot be found, for it has never been lost; it's only the suggestion of the thought-mind which leads or points to its loss. Thoughts are always changing, and this is why you cannot depend upon the thought-mind for the Changeless Experience.[6]

Don't be so egotistically orientated
that the Ideal
is shaped like *you!*

**What you are conscious of
constitutes your experience.
And consciousness of what you are
is your experience.**

Principle is That which is fixed and undeviating and considered to be a State of Consciousness in which all the thoughts that can be attributed to it carry a Deific propensity.

The Ideal must be claimed if man is to be able to engage any semblance of stability in probing a non-gravitational field of conscious awareness, which is the counterweight to the entropic field of the beliefs surrounding materiality and an objective world.

The mind is prepared for dying consciously by being trained to accept the image and likeness of the Divine in a thought structure. When it comes face to face with the Self of transcendency, the mind is already the bride. It is prepared.

You
is the limitation
to pondering an Ideal.

Image will tell you what it looks like;
experience will tell you what it is.[7]

Images
are symbols
of limited conscious experience.

The greatest veil in the temple
that is rent
is the veil of image.

It is so ridiculous to structure your experience upon the
pictures that you have painted about yourself due to
looking in a mirror!

The redeemed imagination enables you to see the picture
through the looking glass and appear to be in that land,
but filled with the wonder at the miracle of clear sight.[8]

Earth
is matter
to the sensory perception.
To conscious knowingness
it is idea.

The only substance to the dream
is the Light
that was never in it.

One moment
swallowed up in Light
is the only moment
there ever is.

Query:
In the Eastern teachings it is said that man must renounce
the world to find God. Is this so?

Answer:
Find God and then tell me what world there is to
renounce!

Query:
How is the world viewed incorrectly?

Answer:
You look at it as if it were not your *own face!*[9]

Your thought-out regions: your world.

The meaning of non-attachment:
not leaving the experience
in the thing
or the thought.

Too many dots give you a picture,
and few there be who ask.

There is nothing wrong with a thought as long as you
know it's a thought. The difficulty lies when you have a
thought and don't recognize it as a thought; you call it
your *condition.*

The mosquito bite is like the world
upon which you stand (the swelling).
In the moment
when there was a lack of attention,
the mosquito bite happened
and you realized your world
was formed. If there is attention,
no mosquito bite, no swelling, no world,
because of the constant awareness which is
sometimes called attention — the evidence
of Self-Realization.[10]

International
is the belief that Being
is scattered.

When you look at history,
see time garmented as thought —
as if Consciousness were in parts!

ere and now, forget about it as earth.

Attention
is the stand that is taken
as the vista of Omnipotence
embraces the sight.

The gift of attention
will be beyond your image.

The conjuring of the average has you
as individuals.
The individual conjuring
has you and your world.

Your world is either a pimple
or a budding rose
according to how you view it.

Event Three

The Truth
isn't in the book,
the Wisdom
isn't in the book,
just as Enlightenment
isn't in the mind.

Various Excerpts

Let It Go

Whatever you do, don't let anyone dream up your past unless in looking at it objectively you can glean a blessing for the now. You mustn't look back on your past! That's all the devil wants you to do. The only value of your past is the fruit it bears to the now. And if it doesn't bear fruit to the now, let it go.

An Abyss Bridged

Query:
Sir, just as the mind would want to conjure up things from the past to trap you, does the mind not also work in a similar way with the future, in doing what my mother has always called "jumping to conclusions"?

Answer:
Yes. The conclusion of any jump should be an abyss bridged. The mind is capable of conjuring up the past to seduce you from being the Presence Now. The mind's suggestion of the future is its ability to hold a promise for tomorrow for those who still believe that Life is in a time-space continuum. The mind is Self-sustained. You see, you'll never destroy your mind; all you do is free it from being what it isn't.

No Footprint in the Sand

The Unfoldment is nothing but a soliloquy, a stream of sound that finds you and carries you on its wave of rhythm onto That Shore where you can stand and walk and leave no footprint in the sand.[1]

Only Secondarily a Person

You are not a man of a nation.
You are a Light experience,
Or a Conscious experience,
And only secondarily a person with a nationality.
You are Conscious Experience
Primarily.

The Phantom of Your Drama

It would seem expedient
For you
Who are engaging the language of freedom
And the liberty becoming the Sons and Daughters of God
To utilize those words of power which are found acceptable
To The State of Liberty,
And to exclude from your language
Those words which could bind you
To the phantom of your drama.[2]

Drop Your Thoughts

Query:
Mr. Mills, is there any form of consciousness other than Divine Consciousness? Is all consciousness Divine?

Answer:
Consciousness as it IS, is Divine. But it *seems* as divided as the thoughts are about it. That's why your thoughts about consciousness are the keys, are the stones on the way to experiencing the Consciousness That IS. The great trick is to be willing to drop your thoughts about Consciousness, for your thoughts about it are changing, and Consciousness never does.

So every thought that's dropped about Consciousness is dropped because Consciousness is right where you thought the thought was!

Query:
That's amazing. In a sense, there are no thoughts as such that can be dropped. You drop your consciousness of the thoughts, or you drop your consciousness of your mind.

Answer:
That's right.

Query:
As soon as the symbol, the thought, or the mind is dropped, then just Consciousness. .

Answer:
Is experienced.

Query:
. . is left.

Answer:
Is experienced. That is why, if you hold my hand and think about it, it's one holding another's hand. However, if there is no thought about it there is only the experience of unity. It's a conscious

experience. In other words, there is no separation between me and thee while **I Am Present.**

The Moment When You Can Fly

Put a value on your schooling. I'm all for schooling. I don't say leave school and behave like jackasses and expect the world to owe you a living. It doesn't owe you a darn thing, but you owe it a tremendous amount, for you're walking on it. You kick it around, you dig it up, you throw the mud around at each other. How many of you take a desert and make it bloom? How many of you cry enough to form even a teardrop?

Use your schooling to the best advantage you can. Look at it objectively as a discipline and then just wait for the moment when you can fly.

Discrimination

Query:
What is it that discriminates?

Answer:
What appears to discriminate is your Divine Status.

Query:
Is that to say, Mr. Mills, that what discriminates is what you are?

Answer:
What discriminates is what you are minus the thought you are that.

You Believe in Miracles?

Query:
Mr. Mills, when a child is born, is it Pure Consciousness?

Answer:
No, it's a dream.

Query:
What's a dream?

Answer:
The belief that you have a child. You're already making it something it isn't. You're trying now, through the mind, to account for something that happened beyond it. Don't try with the rational mind to understand what's happening beyond it.

Query:
It's also an assumption that I am not Pure Consciousness.

Answer:
It's also an assumption that Pure Consciousness could be limited to you, or could be born, or is figured. Pure Consciousness is a mind term, but points beyond the mind.

Wouldn't an awful lot of people love to say that I said children were all dreams? You believe in miracles? I do. And the one that is most important is the one that enables you to see how a dream is the name given to a state that is forever changing. The Light points to That State that is never known or figured to change.

Men, Women, Man

An idea arises from the Source, and that Source is unutterable and unnameable. So is the idea called "man" until he is brought forth and clothed in verbology and thereby limited as *men* and *women*. People get fooled when they talk about something because they project it into an objective sense that seems outside of themselves, which in reality is all within themselves.[3]

When the personality or the "little i" testifies to its condition upon awakening, it's so seldom recognized that it is really testifying to That Source which gives it life. Consequently people fulfill the day experience, unless they really do wake up, in living a fantasy life because they believe that what confronts them as their experience is real and substantial. Yet, that which is substantial, of course, is incapable of deterioration, incapable of annihilation, incapable of any destruction whatsoever, because That which is truly substantial arises side by side with the I.

When your days of meandering become wearisome, the thoughts may then turn in a direction which may lead them Home. The fact which has to be considered is where and how this picture called man and his world arises.

When man born of woman enters upon the earth stage, he is taught to identify through the senses all that confronts him. Through the years he comes to accept the sense testimony as factual and thus is left in a state of distress when there is no unity in the sense-responsive framework which has been built up through his education. When one prompted by his higher Self starts to question the substantiality of his matter world, because it exists through the senses and the language which has been built around the senses, he arrives at a state whereby he almost loses his identity, because with the eventual annihilation of his senses (that is, death) he wonders where he fits into the picture. Yet the senses, being confined to the matter object, cannot really tell an accurate story at all because, premised on matter and belief, they do nothing but build conceptual castles on the sands.

Five Minutes

Are we almost through?
Five minutes?
What we can do with five minutes
Is do five minutes in.
When you think five minutes has passed,
That is a sin. Five minutes
Is only the time it takes
For you to think thought
Into time,
And think you've experienced something.

By having five minutes
You think it less than if you had sixty.
But if you strung nothing
Into time
In the form of five minutes,
Or in the form of one minute,
Or in the form of a thought,
You would find a timeless experience, and that is considered
The Garment
Of Eternity.

If you could look into the momentous
Now,
And not be inundated by any thoughts,
Then you'd be thoughtless.
But you wouldn't be lifeless;
For Life has nothing to do
With a thought.
That's what I mean by
"Shake the hell out of life,"
Because it means to shake out all your thoughts about it.

To think thoughts
And die to them
And find the Thoughtless,
Is to find what is called
"Now."
That's how a prophet could look
Into the past
And into the future,
Because there is no past,
Present or future. It is only thought strung out
That gives either state.
A thought is all wrapped up in the power of projection. The Source
From which it arises
Rescinds all laws of rejection
Or projection
And finds you wrapped
In the garment of a Seamless
Conscious Experience.

The purpose of stopping thought
Is not to realize anything.
It's to be what you really are:
Free.
You can see how quickly I would have to speak
And get right to the point
If I didn't have an hour to do it!

Event Four

See
that you are
conscious
beyond
your intellect's
approval.

Unfoldment
May 23, 1976 Tucson, Arizona

This is the evening of May the 23rd, 1976, and we are speaking from the stone room of the house on the side of the hill in that city which is called Tucson, found in the state of Arizona, one of the many states which is said to comprise the United States of division in the name of America. It is in this state that we are coming to terms with the inner agreement of man's possibilities to unify within the Hall of Knowingness the patterns which have seemed fragmented due to the laws and the processes of thoughts which have no actions to bear to prove a Verity was ever at their source.

The Unfoldment this evening bears in its wake the greetings to all those Centres which are capable of receiving this sound given to a molecular field in which it is stated that a word is heard as a magnetic field is changed,[1] and men and women consider for a moment in awareness the attributes and attitudes becoming One, and having no familiarity or at-easement with two.

The pattern of the days brings each to his place on the calendar of events, which a Soul factor may have sponsored and created, yet how seldom we approach this place and bear witness called knowingness to the situation at hand! The considerations given to everyday experience seem so multitudinous, especially if one feels that it is more fun just to sit and appear to do nothing. But how seldom do we find sitting profitable? And yet, how profitable *is* doing when one is seated in That Spot in the conscious framework that is uncontaminated and unfettered by the hypotheses which would surround a state of education!

Educated jackasses are common today, and no wonder it was so becoming the animal for Jesus to ride it into Jerusalem, because the educated jackass didn't realize that royalty could appear to ride in simplicity. It is interesting how Jesus entered Jerusalem on a jackass, and was greeted by the jackasses, and they all tried to pin a "tale" on him! It is also very interesting to note that when Buddha's mother conceived him, she had a vision of her child riding a white elephant. A little different than the jackass, but each bearing royalty: the elephant a symbol of royalty, and the jackass the disguise of royalty.

It is so interesting that when Gautama married, his father was troubled because his father did not want him to look over the walls and see the world as it seemed to be because he didn't think that Gautama was situated at That Spot, and therefore able to view it in a state of balance. So he fenced him in, and Buddha said, "Don't fence me in." His father said, "I will fence you in, and you will have to see what it is like to live behind these palace walls." So, he got together with a young woman and they had a child and, as you know, the child's name in Indian, when translated into English, means "obstacle." I don't suppose it is ever told to anyone what an obstacle a child is, but if Buddha's child was an obstacle, you can imagine what yours is! Yet, why would you be so afraid to confront an obstacle? There's nothing to an obstacle provided you don't stoop to pick it up. The obstacle course is always one that is contrived so that you can develop muscles in order to jump over or crawl under something that was erected in a natural flow of events.[2]

The best obstacle to a thought-filled mind is the one of perpetuating the thought of limitation, and at the same time the possibilities of Eternality in the form of a child. The children, as you know, have always been highly sought after, one way or another, because they pointed to Eternality in its limited garment. In other words, a child always points to continuity and to bridging the gap between what is called birth and death. So the child is in the sandwich, and bridging the gap between you and yours, and me and mine, and this and That, and never considering that the gap has to be leapt over with no cognitive line.

You see, to understand gives an experience that is a result of an action of the mind coming to terms with a symbol and translating it beyond the word's symbology. That is why, when you have once experienced something beyond these words, it is yours and no one can take it from you. That is the value of this Unfoldment, because the words themselves bear a certain power, so I'm told, that holds your attention, which may have you saying, "Oh my God, I'm bored as hell," or "Oh my God, the Gate is opened and there is Heaven!" And so, you see, you have Heaven and hell sitting on the floor; it all depends upon what is saying which is present. For what is present in all is the mind, and, of course, a mind filled with thoughts is like a road strewn with pebbles. Are you going to stoop to pick them up and throw them at someone else, or are you going to find them polished, as a gemologist would tell you to do, by throwing them into a tumble-barrel, having all their rough edges turned off and then having them so polished that you could use them in a piece of semi-precious jewelry?

This is what the mind is like. It has so many rough edges and it needs somebody like me to cause the thoughts to be flipped around so much that you don't know what's happening, and suddenly you realize something has taken place and you think, "I'll set that because it seems to be a semi-precious situation and one to be worn when I need it to dress up my costume when I'm out on the town!"

Anyone who knows is present; anyone who thinks they know tends to be absent. They say, "Absence makes the heart grow fonder," and it is a lot of baloney that is strung to the lovesick, mature. It doesn't make the heart grow fonder; it's just something to leave your head on the shelf a little longer, you know, so that you don't have to hammer your way through the problem of coming to terms with being single, when you really want to be double. You see, the reason everyone wants to be double is to be single, because, after all, the two shall become One.[3] The only way two can ever become One is to realize that two is One, but seeing itself, forgot that it was looking at itself and considered it another!

One of the causes of the world and its problems is that everyone sees the world in the light of their *own* state of equilibrium, not only in the economy but in the mind systems. If balance cannot be restored, how can the head and heart operate as One with an act that bears a grace? A head by itself can give all kinds of words; a heart by itself can offer a rhythm; but it is when the words bear a rhythm that an act can be performed, and it's almost like bloodless surgery.

No one knows how the Light penetrates, but it is like a laser beam; the penetration is deep, the scientists can control its depth, and we know very well that when it can be utilized and controlled, it can be a marvelous tool in the hands of an educated jackass! The unfortunate part is that the educated jackasses who bring about such marvelous miracles bring about limited miracles, because usually the people who are healed are left with one point still vulnerable: they were physically healed and thought they were made consciously whole![4]

Achilles had his heel, and most people are leashed to a collar of belief with a tag, "I am so-and-so," instead of a flame, "I can only see mySelf, and my collar is only a setting for my precious Jewels of Light." Women wear a choker if they have a neck to show off, and many wear a choker who haven't got a neck to show off, and many appear choked with a choker or without a choker. The interesting part is that a choker of value is set with precious stones and it is cultivated in such a way that the mind is said to be educated to know that this one is gorgeous because it bears a uniqueness, and that one is common because it seems to have had something to do with something else that's been seen before. That's why this is somewhat like a choker to some, this Unfoldment, because it seems to have them on a leash. They say it's wrapped around their thought-like neck, or neck-like thoughts, knowing it's attached to something, but not knowing what. Most of you are led around by the most powerful walker you have — your self-identity tag!

You know, if you go for a walk with your dog, you hold him on a leash in the city so that he won't get run over, or so that he won't go onto other people's property. And yet it is so interesting, when you are out walking, how often do you put your mind of thoughts on a leash so that it won't get run over or so that it won't go onto another person's property? I mean your dog makes a mess here and it makes a mess there. Have you ever considered what your mind is doing when you're walking down the street and having your thoughts right up on someone else's greenery?

It is suggested in Toronto by the Society of — I don't know; we won't bother naming it — but in Toronto it is suggested that if you are out walking your dog, you should carry a paper bag and a little shovel with you, and you know for what purpose! It is so interesting how people can raise such an attention-getter by walking down the street carrying a paper bag with a little spade to take up something dropped. And yet, it would be so marvelous if all people who are walking down the streets had their paper bag and spade and would say, "Oh, I'm so sorry. I dropped the worst mess on your front lawn and I'm here spading it up because I've got to put it into my bag and take care of it myself!"

You see, people who do not know that there is something more to life than just being people think they can think anything they like. But what happens is that sooner or later you have to have something that will free the atmosphere of its swamp-like fragrance.[5]

Now, if you are pursuing a Higher Way, you know very well that it will demand a change. The Higher Way always demands a change for it to be recognized as a Higher Way.

If you are driving in a car and are blindfolded, you have no idea where you are going. This is the way most people go through life. They have their eyes open, but with blindfolds being worn. As soon as something new is seen and not understood, it is generally said, "I don't see it, so therefore it can't be." But when you are blindfolded and being driven in a car, you don't say that the landscape isn't. You just say, "I don't see it." But you can't deny it is.

The purpose of an Unfoldment is not something that you have dreamed up. The purpose of the Unfoldment is to provide an act of attention for a mind on the loose. A mind on the loose is like a great wild horse on the plain, and a great wild horse on the plain has no purpose for you unless you have to hoof it, and then you say, "I must what? Lasso that creature, and then break it so that I can ride it and not have to hoof it any longer." This is what happens in life. People walk and hoof it through life and then decide that they have been taken for a ride. They realize that they have worn out their soles, and, having to buy new shoes, spend a great deal of time considering how to keep a sole together when the leather tops never seem to wear out![6]

This also brings to consciousness the idea that you can be free when you consider that you often say in the morning, "I slept well." The reason you slept well is because you had no thoughts of *you* when you slept. If you did, you had what is called a dream, and sometimes a nightmare, which you feed with your straw-like thoughts! The reason a rest or sleep seems to be satisfying is because there are no thoughts about, and yet there is no thought that I AM not. When you have no thought, you have no sense, and therefore, when you have thought, what arises when you wake up? Thought sense and sense thought, and that's the limit and it's all wrapped up in your bag called *you*.

The head, which we say is wrapped in the shape of a mind, is present for us to use as a tool. Yet it seldom bears the stamp of Eternity because it is left in the realm of limits. This is why in the Unfoldment a Principle is stated. You see, the mind, being undiscriminating, will think anything you give it to think because it lives on thoughts. When the mind hasn't a thought, you're unaware of it. So, the whole point is to feed the mind the thoughts that are commensurate with the Principle,[7] and it will take them and behave accordingly. Then you can appear to be as you seem to be, while you know What IS, in spite of your appearance in what isn't. Got it?

In the Unfoldments, the mind is given a Principle and to the mind this is fantastic. We might say to the mind, "This

is something that you can hang on to whenever you're hungry."
And the mind says, "Great, I'm always starved because if I'm not, I
die for lack of sustenance." So you give it a Principle, and the
Principle is something you find that is undeviating and fixed in
your life experience, just as one (1) is fixed in the realm of
mathematics, yet limited. If the one doesn't see itself, you may call
it two and still be one. But if you fall for the reflection, you may
call it two and find that you're aligning yourself to the reflective
light instead of the direct Light.

Now, if you take a camera (you don't even need a
telescopic lens), all you have to do is open it and face it toward the
sun. What kind of picture do you get when you take a picture of
light? You have no picture. Yet, if you're taking a picture of the
setting sun, as Frank did today, what you are taking a picture of is
a reflection, for the sun has already set. All you are doing is getting
the afterglow of its setting. Everyone worships the setting sun,
which isn't really setting; it's just that the world has turned so
much that the sun is no longer in view, so you have to capture it as
your world turns, not as the sun sets. If you can believe this and
know that the sun isn't setting, that it is just your world that is
turning, why would you not come to believe that the mind is what
is setting as your world appears to turn? It is all lighted by the
Consciousness that doesn't set. Consciousness enables the mind to
appear to set and your world to turn, but It is not touched by
either state.

You say that the moon rises. You know it is the
moon because it wears a silver gown. Sometimes you say, "Darn it,
the night is so dark because there is no moon." What you are
saying is the moon is out of focus as being in the spotlight of the sun;
it is not capable of reflecting sunlight. It is so interesting that
moonlight is not capable of bringing about anything new save a
psychic experience, because it is usually wrapped up in emotional
garments. The sun isn't. You will notice that you are pretty capable
of being active during the day in the light of the sun; it is in the
light of the moon that you start wondering about all your satis-
factions and your dissatisfactions. During the day you don't have
time to wonder. You must be about your business, which is what?

It is usually evidencing what the mind has been skilled to do.

Now, what if your mind accepts a Principle and becomes skilled in taking a plane before anyone else, and appears to lead the way? When you see a man going to the airport, you may be seeing the pilot. Yet, it is fascinating the price you pay to fly when you don't know, only by hearsay, the credentials of the pilot. But you trust your life to him, and you trust your life to a mechanical contrivance. And when you don't you do something about it.

Several years ago I was going to New York and it came time for the airplane to depart and everyone started to get fidgety, making way to the exit in order to board the plane. I remained in my seat because I felt intuitively something was wrong. Everyone got up, and then an announcement came saying, "We're very sorry to announce that this flight will be delayed for about forty-five minutes." So, after feeling that the plane wasn't right, I identified the plane and knew it to be an intrinsic part of my all-encompassing Divine Nature. I freed it from being being thought in terms of a fuselage and stabilizer and a pilot and a contrivance of transportation. I dwelt in this state of awareness, and when we got on the plane there was a seat vacant beside me and I beckoned to the stewardess and asked her to come over for a minute and sit down. I said, "Tell me, what happened?" She said it was the strangest thing. The craft had taxied up to the place of departure when suddenly the pilot felt there was something wrong, but he didn't know what it was. He felt it so strongly that he asked that the plane be overhauled before taking off. She said, "You know, sir, when they took it back they found a malfunction in one of the engines." Isn't that interesting?

You see, the plane, the gate, the delay, and the correction (the healing) and all the acts that took place are likened unto the steps that you can engage in entering a higher level of action through engaging principles that support each level until you know the Pilot, and *are* the Pilot of your own ship of consciousness. As long as you have it camouflaged in the shape of a body, under the control of a mind, you must be sure that it is schooled in the Temple of the Light, because this is where the sacrifice must be made.

Remember, a sacrifice is a loss, and you have made no sacrifice if it isn't a loss. A loss is only a loss to the one who is sacrificing, because after the sacrifice has taken place, it has become a gain. It is like emptying a cup; you cannot receive something in a cup if it is already full. It's like the tea service, you know, the story about the Tea Master who had somebody come for tea. The Tea Master filled the guest's cup to the brim with tea, and then still kept pouring. The tea went all over the table and down onto the floor. His guest said, "The tea is spilling all over the place." And the Tea Master said, "Yes. It is like you. You are so filled, how can you receive anything that I have to give?" It is in the attitude of being emptied of opinions that you may find a fragrance fills the air.[8]

Consciousness is fundamental and what you are conscious of constitutes your experience. But a mind is not Consciousness; a mind is like the film in a camera. When it can't take a picture of the sun .. *that is Consciousness!* You say, "I can't see the body of the sun, and yet I took its picture and it just ruined my film!"

Now, if you are demanding proof of the validity of a conscious state, you are limiting that conscious state to the level of your proof which you are demanding. If somebody asks you to heal their big toe and you heal their big toe, they will think you're a big toe healer. And if you have a bad headache and somebody asks you to heal their bad headache, then you will be known as a bad headache healer. You will soon be called a healer and what happens? The great point of weakness is this obstacle: that you stoop to heal.

The great weakness of Jesus was that he stooped to heal as proof of his power. The one healed only called him a leader, a walker on the Way. In other words, Jesus walked the Way with those whom he had healed, or who had witnessed the healings, and they became his followers. After he left, all they could do was talk about his healings and his miracles, and they could do little to elucidate the Teachings of the Transcendental School of the Masters.

This is why the churches are stuck with the books of the Bible, which are nothing but fragments given as remembrances, in many cases, of those who wrote hundreds of years after Jesus passed. The fragments of the lost gospels which have been found in the caves are not published, and they perhaps won't be, because if they are published they will reveal without a shadow that what was termed the High Teachings of Jesus had nothing whatever to do with a priesthood, or with a church established in His name.

To be a minister of the gospel is one thing, but to be a practitioner of the Light is to be the evidence of a conscious state in which no limits are recognized. We are concerned with seeing the states (mental and geographical) and say, "They are united, and yet why have they no power?" It's because each thinks in terms of his condition, of his state and its legislature, and not in terms of the Government which must be upon His shoulders so that the appearance of diversity shall fade out in the Light of the Unification of the Christ.

The world has always been wondering about Oneness in the face of multiplicity, and the world has always been pondering the paradox of humanity and divinity. As long as you are in the realm of wondering, let the miracle be that you shall see that in the State of Realization, the human or the divine has nothing whatsoever to do. . with a cat on a hot tin roof! ((The sound of an animal scampering across the roof had just been heard. Ed.))

If you find that the animal nature has climbed to that place where it says it can walk on the roof of your accomplishment, you know very well that it is only the first step on the way to the stars, because the animal nature left in the grass of a mental garment brings forth its own kind, and that's one of limits. The nature that is freed through the conscious appropriation of attitudes and attributes commensurate with what is said to be beyond itself and termed Divine will soon be able to blossom in your garden, and you will say you have seen how the desert shall bloom as the rose and find that in the wake of the Rose, only its invisible gown of fragrance is experienced.

It is so interesting how we trust our life to our mind. And we have pilots: ministers, priests, teachers who say, "Worship me because I am the pathway to your freedom." Few will say, "Learn to structure your own ship of Soul and find yourself the Pilot of your ship." You have to fill your sails with the Might of Omnipotence. If the oil pressure is down and the red light goes on, know that this is pointing to the lack of consecration, the lack of patience, the lack of devotion and the lack of obedience. When these are met you will find that the light turns green and then you can say, "Ah yes, the Gate is opened, the plane is taken, for I know that the wings of the Angel of the Lord have gone before me, and all the lights are green."

Green is the great colour of the fecund state, it is the great colour of balance, and it is the great colour that gives freedom a happy way if you can find that the state commensurate with an Ideal has nothing to do with the thoughts of *you*. Claim your Ideal by thinking not in terms, but in words or ideas of such grandeur that your mind says, "They are simply beyond me," and at that moment you know they are already part of your trousseau of Light. It works!

This is very simple this evening because of Sandra and I don't want it to be so far out that Sandra or her mother and father, Donna and Frank, will be too far lost in wondering what in hell I'm talking about, because you know, as I said before,

*I came to bring hell to those who doubt that a setting may
    be found.*
*Why, you may take your hammer and find a pavé of
    diamonds abounds.*
And you may say in a moment of Light, "Why the green

has become as planned
The platform upon which I stand and appear to come unto
man."

I came to bring hell to those who think that the Divine
can be claimed in thought;
I came to bring hell to those who think that the Divine
can be thought out—rot!
I came to bring hell to those who think that doubt is part
of the Way;
I came to bring the power to roll the pebbles of your
rock-like day.

But you can also wear your gown of blue and know that
the Virgin did too,
For she did carry the Child of Might, and she named it
Jesus for you.
And then you know as He rode the Way, and a donkey
was claimed in the Act,
Why, the palm fronds were spread before the donkey, and
oh, what a tale was that!

Few did know that the palm fronds pointed to the
accomplished plan
Of subduing the thought-like mind of time so that it
would be prepared for the man of Man.
And then in the walk and in the stroll up to the Gate of
time,
You called it the Gate of Jerusalem and you said, "The
Gate is opened and it will blow my mind."

And then Gautama, who became frustrated with his place,
Looked right over the walls of time made by the king, his
father, in place
Of the transparent Wall of Light through which he could
see the fact
That all of the suffering and turbulent mobs which
surrounded his place, his palace, his act
Were really there to see it come to pass away in the Light,

And he said, "I'll have to claim that tree and find how I
      may become one with its root and branch of
      Light."

So he sat and he pondered and he stilled the thought and
      the tree, it started to bloom,
And they all started to find this man and they said, "A
      Buddha! Swoon!"
And then, when they got over the fact of His presence,
      they said, "Oh, he's just another man."
And he sat right under the Bodhi-Tree and he said, "I have
      no gift to give to man."

And then he was asked so many things, and the Truth
      sealed his lips,
Because he knew very well it had nothing to do with any
      thought of a mister or a miss.
And when he was asked what could he say, it's stated that
      "Happiness Is" sprung from his lips,
And then some said, "I'm miserable, so I'll have to become
      a disciple of his, and amiss."

What a misguided act is truly found in the way of trying
      happiness on for size,
Because happiness is a grace, you see, that really does
      blow the mind.
Happiness has nothing to do with a thought in your head
      at all;
That's how you deck it up and tell a Rick or a Tara about
      the ball.
Happiness is a state of Grace, for it comes when the mind
      is still,
And that's why you say, "Oh, I slept so well," for it had
      nothing to do with me, for me did not enter into
      this still.

So the picture was framed, and so you find when the Light
      was bright as planned
That the film on the negative was there as it is, and not a

print of you as a man.
And the only verdict you found in the Light was that "I
slept well in this day
All because the sense of me was not found on this plane
arrayed."

Now, when you pick up your body and all your thoughts
of time,
You may say, "Oh my God, what a hell of a way I've got
to work and ride on the jackass of time!"
But you can do it, for you come to see that if your work
in the world is to be,
You can appear to be hoofing your way around and
claiming the Power of Deed.

So you claim your horse on the prairie in sight and you
lasso it with the ring as planned,
For the ring is what you find when you form a Principle
and circle: Man.
And then you take your mind, the horse, and ride it
through the plane,
And then you come to tether it at the frontier where the
Infinite is gained.

Did you know that the Infinite is the last post of the
mental realm of Light?
Because what have you got beyond that spot unless the
experience is Light?

So it's been mighty fun to see you, and it's been an easy
talk,
But it's wrapped up with a ribbon and tied with a bow
and it's frocked
All in a gown of promise, wrapped up with a boutonniere
of Light;
And if you can get dressed up in time, you might find the
ball in sight.

And may you come to the ball in sight and find as you

come to see
That the Prince is there awaiting, if you are dressed in
deed.
And then you will know the meeting, and then you will
know the fact
That the music played and the rhythm was heard, and
although your feet were touching the ground,
You will know in the Act of Being I AM, your Soul has
left the ground.

That's how you can seem to walk and play and have a ball of time, for you know that you can throw it out and bring it back, all because you never left home, although you appeared a pilgrim of time. If it means anything to you, great. If it means nothing to you, great. If it means anything, let it point to That Which IS beyond anything that it means.

It's been one hour on the dot. The people from San Francisco arrive on Tuesday and it should be an interesting week. Frank and Donna and Sandra leave on Tuesday and it might be nice if you could have a class tomorrow night and have them with you. Every Unfoldment is such that the note of harmonic significance is discerned, but the embellishment will always be woven according to those present in the room. It's a very different frequency because they are present, because they have not been here before; but having been here now, the next time will appear very different.

It is so simply given, and yet so laden with precious jewels. Since my nephew Frank is a great lover of jewels, I thought I would cover his way with them and let him think that they were just pebbles. That's what I have given in the Unfoldment — that the pebbles are those states of thought, wrapped in doubt, which are not transparent. A precious jewel is precious because of its hidden fire which can be released under the accuracy of a gem cutter who knows how to cut the stone to reveal it, and thus find how a star is born! The tumbler, like the tumbleweed, is very symbolic, and only as the symbols take on meaning beyond what you think, do they carry a power that transports you right in to the

Keeper of the Jewels.

It states in one of the old, old hymns, "When He cometh, when He cometh to claim all His jewels, precious jewels, precious jewels, the gems of His Crown." These Crown Jewels are the positive centres. I have also talked about the negative centres this evening, of what men and women call the dragon or the kundalini. The kundalini is the great fire that rises in the spine, and the centres that are activated along the spine by it are called the negative centres. No teacher of the High Light works through raising the kundalini voluntarily. They work through the positive centres of the Crown. As each one of these is lighted, it becomes a precious "Jewel".

In order to enter the state of the Christ Realization of the Self, these Jewels have to be set. When Jesus was taking his Enlightenment through the senses, he experienced it as the crown of thorns, as long as he personalized it. The work in the tomb was really that time when he freed himself from the personalization of the divine attributes commensurate with the Realized State called the Christ. It pointed to every man's freedom, not to one person's freedom. That is the great paradox: how in God's name was Jesus the human, and the Christ the Divine? It has been the fight of the clergy for centuries. That's why they are still clergy. They are arguing over the human and the Divine when it doesn't enter into the question when the Crown is set with precious stones. It's all Realized.

There is so much to this Unfoldment, but there is to every tale, you know, even when you're blindfolded. At birthday parties they used to play "Pin the Tail on the Donkey." It was so funny to see everyone, but I never could get too much fun out of it because every time I saw anyone blindfolded trying to pin the tail on the donkey, I wanted to jab the ass with a pin! Fascinating, isn't it? The games we play, and we think we are having a birthday party.

Most birthdays, as Dr. de Lange once said, would stop being celebrated in the old way if you started to think of them as death days, because as long as you think you are aging, you are dying. "Aging," Dr. de Lange said, "is death in slow motion."[9] This is why it is so imperative for you to be filled with the thoughts that are termed youthful, because they carry the energy and the vitality that can bring purpose to an Unfoldment, for the giver of the Unfoldment has no other purpose than that which is pertinent unto the Self.

I don't have to prove anything, and this has been the salt in the wound of many of those who have wanted proof. The proof of a miracle is not in the healing of a toe; it's in That State of Consciousness which leaves the toe where it belongs and restores the thought of reverence to its rightful place in the Kingdom of the Light.

Query:
At class the other evening there was a question brought up concerning imaging, and I've been sitting here attempting to put it into a question, and I'm unable to. I was wondering..

Answer:
Why don't you just talk about it for a minute. Don't put it into a question. Perhaps it doesn't need an answer. Perhaps you just have to hear yourself speak and you'll find you have the answer.

Query:
Well, I have been unable..I don't want to start that way. I have been viewing this work in the light of..

Answer:
Thank you. In the Light. That is where you might as well put the period. You didn't say to the camera, when you exposed it to the sun, "I expect to see an image." You got it. There wasn't any, in terms of limits. Don't image with limits. The only point of a picture is to hold in remembrance an experience until you know the Eternality of Light. The picture book of the mind is made up of stills. The point is to come to the Source and find what is called the Peace, and the Be, and Still. Peace, Be, Still. Peace Be Still. Still Be Peace. Be Still is Peace.

78

Thoughts are rampant, like the wild horse on the prairies. That's why you ride them. You don't let them ride you. Image after an Ideal. The great legacy and faculty of Nathanael-Bartholomew, one of the disciples of Jesus, was that of imaging. Imagination is very important. But imaging in terms of *you* and your world and your thoughts about it is the limited world. It's the divided world, and it's the starving world. This is nothing to be peeped at, you see. It is a very deep and penetrating experience, and the mind and its thoughts will never get it. It's only when the thoughts of the mind can be brought under the Reins of Power that you can ride it and find that your destination is Home.

Query:
Is the taming of the thoughts, then, through the method of comparing them to the Ideal?

Answer:
That's one of the ways. But the best way to still the mind is to find a thought and chase it. Chase a thought and you will find you have no mind to be still. A watched pot never boils. It's the same thing with the mind. A watched mind can't be found because it ceases to boil. Subdue the mind by watching it. The mind, you see, is only the name that you give to all the thoughts that you have about your world and you.

> *I'm wearing my red coat of fire, and I hope you've been*
> *held in its light.*
> *And I hope, as you've caught the meaning of this Wesak*
> *Festival of the Buddha Light*
> *That the planes are filled with the magic and the wonder*
> *of a Redeemed Imaging Might.*
> *Always dream true to the Realm of Power; dream true to*
> *the Power of Might,*
> *And find that you sleep not, but are awake, and open and*
> *read your Manuscript of Light.*

You must read your own scrolls by freeing them from a black disc of reflective might and wait for the Sun to shine on them. In a room that has been filled with darkness for a thousand years, you only need one little candle to see what is in it, and the need of dusting.

Event Five

Who has seen
the garment of the wind?
save worn by the leaf,
worn by the Word
and carried on the wave
of communication.

When the bow let the arrow fly,
who knew its direction?
But the wind yielded
to its purposeful point.[1]

Your gown is the web that you wear to support those who
need to see unearthly beauty and still be able to say, "It
appeared unto me when the dew was *still* on the roses."
See?

A snowdrift showed, for those who doubt, a form of the
passing wind.

When the tree bows toward your house,
remember the wind
is greeting you impersonally!

Every hair in follicle
stands up straight when breezes frolic.
When no hair moves in place,
you describe the follicle traced.

Expectation
is the garment a thought can wear
as it approaches the pyre of Light.

With the action of the Breath,
sit with the *air* of expectancy.

Meditation is mechanical, just like the piano. You use the mechanics of meditation, and beyond it — the Music of the Spheres!

Query:
Does it matter in meditation whether the eyes are open or closed?

Answer:
Yes, it's easier to keep them closed. You have enough thoughts about what you don't see — I can't imagine how many you would have if you opened your eyes and thought you saw as you were trying to meditate. You might as well pull the blinds on the suggestion that outside of you is the world!

A thought watched
is a thought stilled.

The Watcher is One
and holds you in embrace.

You think *you* are conscious.
You limit it.

Attention
is paying homage to the
Invisible Watcher
of the field of thought.

Query:
The most startling experience of my meditation is that
after finishing I felt as though I stepped out of an airplane
and into a car.

Answer:
That would be startling if you thought that Consciousness
were different in either case!

Query:
Mr. Mills, what is memory?

Answer:
The suggestion that what is known could be forgotten.

The only thing that identifies you with a painful condition is thought.

A thought fanned to its highest is a thought purified of a thinker.

> *You* is the noise of doing
> and *I* is the Soundless not-doing,
> and appearing to have done..
> and do.

> As long as you are trying
> to silence your mind,
> you are creating your mind.

> As long as you are trying to empty
> your mind,
> you are already full
> of your own conceit!

Fermata's Hall

It is the Pause within the unfolding pattern of design,
Be it a composition in music or a pattern in Mind;
There must be the Pause to fashion the form,
So that the idea of music may be borne
On the wings of sound
To all who abound
In the regions where it can be found.

Its melody is brought into the now
By the inspiration which supports the Cause
In order that harmony may fill the Pause
Wherein man may find the rest
And taste a moment of blessedness.

The Pause Divine fulfils the Law
Wherein Principle is the only Cause,
United with the rhythmic power
Creates for man within its tower
The joy of finding all that made
The cadence chords within Heaven staid.

The chord which lost its way in time
Is found by man when so inclined
To rest within the Base Divine
On which the chords are formed in Mind.

They're staid, they're set for one who sees
The pulse behind Reality;
They are not free to move about
At whim of fancy or of doubt.

They are set in pattern all,
So that they may ever fall
Into the realm of opened thought,
Which becomes enraptured wrought
As the Music of the Spheres
Holds thee bound within its reels.

There's no separation for one who knows
The joy of Being with the Doh
Which was the first note ever struck
Within the realm where Man and God
Set beside the bell which wrought
The Tone Sublime which filled the hall
When God and Man did fill the call
To rest, to pause, to strike the bell
And to declare that all is well.

Stop and rest if weary be,
For in this place beside the sea
It is home, called Doh to you,
For 'tis wrought for all who do.

So when daylight comes to you,
Then you'll know the Doh and do,

For its sound envelops you.
Listen well within this Hall,
For the Sound that does not fall
On the one serene, at peace,
Who with the rhythmic I doth meet.

'Tis the Silence of the scribe
Who would write as one abides,
And fulfils the need for all
Who hear the music as outside the Hall.

But when he enters Fermata's Hall,
Then he'll know the soundless Pause
Beckoning one to come inside
Where the rhythmic I abides.

**Only thought
freed from the body
enables you
to fly.**

Self-awareness can't be divided
from awareness
which is the Self.

The Source is the Substance
to any thought about it.

In the stilling of your thoughts,
may you see the flight of the swallow
and consider the intent and purpose
of a goal and an aim
when you would die to the choiceless choice
of Being what you are.
It is in the flight from sense to non-sense
that you realize the insubstantiality of
what appears to be the substance
of your earth.

Your I AM, you might say, is the sound equated with the
cry or the chant of Light, for it is forever ringing down the
corridors, over the pines, over the fountains, and
supporting the birds in their call.

An age without wonder
is an age with no miracle.

The demand of any age
is to be freed from being
thought happening.

Every thought
that is employed in Love is work.
Every thought
that is employed in selfishness
is unemployment.

Employment is the office open
for knowingness in action.

Query:
Why am I myself and not somebody else?

Answer:
Because your I is a direct experience, and someone else's, a
suggested one!

A person doesn't unfold;
he folds up!

Thoughts properly used
become the language
of awareness.

When the thought is seen
for what it is,
there is still the thought,
but no bound thinker.

The I AM
permits man to assume
an "I am" identity,
but the I AM
isn't in the identity.

Duplicity is the result
of one falling
for seeing itself.

The mind can receive
only when it is empty
of its thought
satisfaction.

When you think in private,
your action is public!

The thought world knows yesterday, today
and tomorrow;
the conscious world experiences only Now.

When the hand is opened, there is your world.
When the hand is shut, there is your limitation.
When the hand gestures in the Grace of Love,
There is a symbol for the Promise from above.

Query:
You can't put one coat on every man and expect it to fit.

Answer:
You can put the one coat of Consciousness on every man
and let him cut his own garment!

Everything that is left over
after your thinking has
stopped
is Life.

It is impossible
to finish off thought,
because to finish off thought
is to begin with it![2]

To be conscious
transcends your thoughts
of what consciousness is.

One thought
thought to be yours
is the wall between Heaven
and earth.

It's silly to be chasing a thought
unless it is to its Source!

Event Six

*The miracle
of Conscious Experience
bypasses the bars of time
and enables you to fulfill
a calendar of engagements
as a natural sequence
of Holy Events.*

Unfoldment
August 31, 1975 Toronto

The purpose of being present in this number is to bring unto the band of attention the need for adoption of those means and methods whereby you may align yourself unto the Self that is exalted as God is, and is said to be in His Heaven and all's right with the world.

So, if it is considered that all is right with the world, you can see that that standpoint is fallacious. For all is not right with the world if God is in His Heaven, for you have separated yourself, perhaps, and put God in His Heaven and left yourself on earth as a wanderer! And if you find your world's all right, are you being satisfied with your wandering and the world in its orbit? Or are you trying to engage the means whereby you can stop your world and get off and on at will?[1] If God is in His Heaven, what kind of a world could God be experiencing if it is declared "all right"?

If God could make such a declaration, he must have made it with the intent that there was someone below to accept this statement as a point of faith. For if the world is changing, so must God be, and I would not be seduced into saying that all's right with the world if God is changing as it seems to be!

This is why, you might say, a world in His image is not found in yours. And this is why, you might say, the world doesn't owe you a living, for if you think you are one with it, it needs your support in its death throes. And how can you support the dying? By dying at a slower rate of speed![2]

The purpose of you being here, let us say, is on behalf of the world's population. You are tipping the scales on the fulcrum of Light into a balanced state for the entire concept of world. The Action that will redeem the world from its imbalance is the Action that is found when men and women are freed from the story of a successless life experience.

To have success is considered remarkable, and not to have success is considered marked; but the remarkable situation is to find that a success story is never written about a partial story. It has to do with the totality of experience when freed from experiment.[3]

To experiment with success may have it appearing in different areas of your life. But what area does Life occupy? And if you are to have success, you know very well that to be successful, you must initiate. And if you have no initiative, how will you be able to enter the rank and file of the Initiated?[4] To consider the Initiation is to consider what it is to be at the Root of Creative Might, having been adopted by said Event. God IS. Man IS. World IS. That IS. Where are you?

An Initiate is one who is able to begin anew because he has conformed to the prescribed means of entering the Room where the act of beginning and commencing anew is held in Light. And the whole purpose and intent of the action is to enter That State of Awareness whereby the world and its limitations are seen in the Light of a living God experience, and no longer held as a God-like experiment (thinking in terms).

You see, the ramifications that come to your consciousness as you consider your world and its plight are many. If you consider your world as outside yourself, you have created the need of having to come to terms with an objective creation. If you have seen the success story of another in the obvious success of a world action, then you have only the act, his action or her action to remember until yours is experienced.

The act of accomplishment, wearing the garment

of success, is an involuntary happening because the one has been selfless in the engagement of abstract exercises[5] so that no objectification can get in the way when the Mind of God is freed from the mind of men and walks in the realm of a conscious experience, dictating unto the pen, and unto the fingers, and unto the tongue those sounds commensurate to His story, unsung in the world, but a dithyramb of significance in the stellar sphere of accomplishment.

To chant the praises of Self-accomplishment is inevitable, even in act, when the Self accomplished is the Act involuntarily offered. The work comes when you consider yourselves separated, and in parts, which is the original sin.

The picture-book of the mind is giving you you and your world. The picture should be so sketched that you see, in your tracings upon the tissue of time, the world and its possibilities in the Light of a Cosmic Knowingness. The world freed from a thought structure is universally garmented in an energy commensurate with Light. A mind freed from thoughts is one given into the act of a selfless action.

Love is the Power that enables God to be a living experience, your world levitated into your hand, and your head found to be dazzling with points of Light, due to the opening of the door. The Robe of the Immaculate Righteousness is only found when Love is the garment in which your world and your God are wrapped. Now, to put on the Robe of an Enlightened State is to put on the Robe that sees no man in need of Enlightenment. And to be in a state where you see men and women in need of Enlightenment has you in their midst preparing the crucifixion.[6]

There is but One Principle and One Mind as Act. This is all you need to know to engage the solitary act of technical practice. To be a success in music demands that you be a success in abstract exercise done in the seclusion of your own room. To develop a technique enables you to evidence such discipline that *you* die out as I come forth. And when I come forth, I will come forth bearing a symbol that is capable of a synchronistic appearance to the mind, but a Light experience when freed from mindfulness.

When it is understood, there is no thought of trying to experience, because often the understanding is itself the experience. Up until that point it has only been knowledge, and knowledge is the result of experiment. Experience can point to the intuitive act freed from the programming of a mind based on principles. There are all kinds of principles underlying the life structure of the world and its inhabitants; but there is only One Principle that lights up all of your acts. In the Principle, find freedom.

The only purpose of being purged is to bring about a catharsis of the soul, which has nothing to do with how you think. The catharsis of the soul is a grace that enables the feeling of Being I AM to be freed from the contamination that I am what I think I feel. If I am what I think I feel, then I am what I think I am in feeling. And if I am what I think I am in feeling, then in feeling I think I am. If I am I think in feeling, then I am feeling in thought, and **I AM** not in thought! I AM is a sound that a word may wear with meaning, and means to bring about your Self face to face. A life filled with Glory is like a word filled with meaning, and a word without meaning is nothing but fodder for the cannon of your mind!

I wonder if wonder could be present if **I** were not. *You* are no wonder! Your success is no wonder; your *lack* of success is the conundrum! If you are a success, it is because **I AM** more than you think I am. And if I AM more than thought, then My success is not open to your speculation about My experience; for My experience is one with my knowing intuitively that the Feeling of Being I AM is capable of moving through the door in a dance of Power.7

To feel the rhythm of the dance is to know that God is alive, but to feel it in your foot may leave it on the floor, and you might say, "My feet feel the rhythm but my head is so minus this impulse that I haven't the heart to go on!" And as I said recently up at the lake, the head could be likened unto a hammer left on a shelf; what good is it if you don't have the heart to take it and bring it into an act commensurate with the witnessing box of the Age in which you find yourself? If you know an experience, then you must behave as a knowing experience.

How many greet the day in the Conscious Light of a continuing wonder experience? I wonder at the calendar that says one day has passed to another. I wonder at the miracle that I can see someone apparently new and know them Now. I wonder at being in an auditorium, and seeing it filled in Truth.

If you think you have a purpose in your life action that is pertinent unto your peevish self, then know that you are in the realm of no wonder, and only in the realm of the ramification surrounding all the sponsored suggestions of time. The point of our being here is to hold in remembrance who and what, where and how it shall come to pass that you shall find yourself wearing the Robe.

"If with all your hearts ye truly seek Me, ye shall surely find Me," thus saith the Law, or the Lord. "If with all your hearts," for the heart must be the source of the poetic rhythm and wonder, and the head must be able to testify to that signature in which the composition unfolds from the Source that is undifferentiated. Each man and woman shall write his own cadence as he changes his garments.[8]

In the act of being Present, be absent from your thoughts and find how **I AM** the Source of wonder. How can salt, water, chalk, protoplasm, or slime[9] ever testify to the Immutable and Immortal? The miracle of Conscious Experience bypasses the bars of time and enables you to fulfill a calendar of engagements as a natural sequence of Holy Events.

The whole purpose of life is to LEAP![10]
And in the leap find yourself in the lap of the Sage, and the fragrance the evidence of success. Remember! A rose has a fragrance, and so do its petals when they are brought to the ashes.

I tell you now, it is an ever-recurring accent of wonder that a Phoenix[11] may arise, and man may be seen walking o'er the Bridge of the Rainbow.

Query:
Mr. Mills, I am not asking for a definition, or even an iron-clad answer, but I have been waiting to hear something of a formula for Self-Realization, that is, Realization of the Deity.

Answer:
Yes. Well, the best way to find it (that is, the experience), is to free it from the thought form, see it as the Source of the thought form, and in experiencing the Source of the thought form, find your Self unformed and yet formed as your experience. *Go to the Source of the thought form and find in the leap that I AM All.* You will never lose your Identity, although you may appear to be so transformed that others may not know you!

Query:
Mr. Mills, last week you spoke about time and, if I understood correctly, said that what we call the past or the future is simply the Now clothed in a thought garment.

Answer:
Yes. The past, the present and the future freed from thought is Now.

Query:
In the same way then, sir, is it possible to do away with the notion of others and me?

Answer:
It is possible to do away with the *notion* of others and me because in the Now I AM All. What appears as others and me are only those acts offered unto the stage of time waiting for space and time to dance together and leave only a figured rhythm to point to the suggestion that a figure has anything other than an illegitimate life because it changes; it has only been a suggestion pointing to the Unfigured which *is* the mark of significance.

It is a grace of the Unfigured that a figured act could appear to happen and appear to be marked for time, by time, and in time for those who ride on the wave of expectation into the harbour beyond all chance.

Query:
Mr. Mills, in viewing what appears as others as not being outside myself, what makes a Dianne a Dianne, and a Bonnie a Bonnie?

Answer:
Oh, I'm not saying the others aren't outside you. They are. But to break the suggestion that there is no meaning in their appearance is why you look within to see no division. And you will realize that there is no division because the One Garment that is present in every so-called case is the Garment of Consciousness which you will cut according to your need. You are not annihilating what appears as the world; you are just appreciating how it is all wrapped up in the One Garment or Robe of All-inclusiveness.

Query:
Mr. Mills, is the only way to go to the Source to be the Source?

Answer:
The only way to go to the Source is to forget it. When you know that a city is your destination and you go to it, you forget it..you live in it! Go, and experience!

The whole value of these Unfoldments is in the pointing. For each feels within himself that happiness IS, that God IS, World IS, I AM That I AM IS. This is innate! To like or dislike me has nothing to do with it. What a miracle that you can say, "I wonder at my own wonder." Never stop wondering at your own wonder! It is no wonder that you wonder until you experience what is the Light to the miracle and the wonder, and I points to that. It's direct! If you make it circuitous, it is only because you like to be on a circuit route with the wheel of hope not even whispering, but left as a pie to be cut into parts according to the demands of life action.

Thank you for your presence and for all you have done around your act of offering unto the landscape the evidence that you were there when the birds watched your act in order to relate unto Jonathan. Some can fly with no danger right into the thicket of time and weave a nest of promise for those who would crack the egg of suggestion and find the world in their hand as their head would dance in the rhythm of the act. Aren't the roses beautiful?

Event Seven

It is so ridiculous
to be searching for
Enlightenment;
it's as if God were not
Omnipresent!

The Christ

In simplicity,
Power rode the Way.

A donkey
ridden in knowingness
bears a Prince
of the realm Unknown.

The Christ is that transforming power which enables man
to fulfill his destiny upon this sphere of action without the
pangs of suffering the delusion of death or birth.

The Truth of Being
has always been present;
it's only been accented
by those who love.

The Christ feature of Jesus
finds no man doing
from the standpoint
of personal power.[1]

The tomb experience is really a *you* experience. The Jesus experience is a mental experience. The Christ is Conscious Birth.

Spiritual pursuits
is only the name given
to some condition of consciousness
which is less identified with the objective.

The Christ doesn't keep his thought filled
with Life, Truth, and Love;
the Christ is
Life, Truth, and Love!

The Christ is the Grace which descends that enables you to recognize your Divine Essence.

What is a sermon? An unfoldment with no intent or purpose but to rejoice in the fullness of Being.

Today the crucifixion is not on the cross; it's in the mind. And that's where you take unto yourselves thoughts that you think. You see, thought is a strange thing; it's pivotal in nature, for it can appear to belong to the world of limitation and it can appear to point to the Realm that is Infinite. It is paradoxical. The state commensurate with Realization has nothing to do with trying to bridge the gap between this and That. It's done by a leap, an intuitive leap, and you can't *think* yourself into it. The reason you are using thoughts is to prepare a springboard, where at the right moment you can have a realization and know it has happened!

The Christ Consciousness
is forever present
but not experienced
because men think through the terminology
of a material framework.

The Great Tide of current event is the rhythm of the
Christ Eternal. It is forever repeating, and yet never
happening more than once.

The Christ is that Divine Power which enables an incorrect
thought pattern to be moved to a correct standpoint and
found commensurate to the Body of Man in the image and
likeness of his Ideal, called God.

Mary:
the state of consciousness
receptive to miracle.

A Master
is one who has gained
the right of silence,
and performance if requested.

To be great, be a servant.
To be a fool, be thought a master!

The Promise of the Age is that all men shall be Light, and that the world shall be Light. Realize that you of yourself can do nothing but *I Am* a miracle worker. You will then find God-Being evidenced in your actions of love, tenderness, and compassion, one to another. There is none other than the Self that is simply Divine that walks forth from the sepulchre which you call your entombed mentality. The Age of Light bears the power of eradicating a faulty thought pattern and exchanging a death sentence for Eternal Life.

The purpose of living
is to die
to the suggestion of being
a personal liver
and find
Life
Lived.

Nothing could have been resurrected
had it truly died.

If you think
you are living in a body,
you are carrying around your own
sepulchre.

Willingness to die
evidences itself as enquiry.

The only thing that can die
is the thought that Life is limited.

The only decision that you ever have to make is to die to
the suggestion that you are not already the directed action
of the Light.

Figure

If the body is to have an identity at all, you must be conscious of it, and what you are conscious of constitutes your experience. You see, consciousness is fundamental, and if consciousness is fundamental you know that it is only in consciousness that you can experience body. You, I, or anyone does not really experience a physical or a material *body* as such. We are actually, in fact, only aware of the *idea* body. The notion that the body is material is itself an idea! The body is a manifestation of a series of ideas, a conscious experience, and people mistake it and believe it to be material.

With the realization that the body is really a series of ideas (that is, a conscious experience) comes also the awareness that the ideas which constitute the experience of body are contained in Mind. Mind always evidences itself as consciousness. That's why we say that consciousness is fundamental, because as long as you are conscious you will always be embodied. You will always have that body which is necessary for you at the time you seem to need it. It will be one that fulfills its function wherever you seem to be.

The victory
of the grave
is mistaken
identity.

Query:
Is there a reason why man has chosen this manifestation of a physical body for his action on this supposed plane of existence?

Answer:
Find first the proof of the manifestation; then you'll know the answer.

*The greatest gift
that can be given to man
is the ability to see
through the solidarity that confronts him
and find it transparent.*

All that you find embodied
is a limited sense
of what Consciousness is.[2]

The body proves its own purpose by showing you that there is more to it than meets your eyes. You are aware of your body as a conscious experience. This conscious experience becomes the Living Body when you cease identifying with the evolutionary body and find the Body That IS.

You don't have to prove Love.
Your very existence
is the evidence of Love.

Query:
What is revelation?

Answer:
Bringing to cognition what is already known but buried
beneath the thoughts of a thinker.

The whole purpose of Realization
is to find that everything
that you thought was,
isn't,
and everything that you didn't think,
IS.

The One Bell
would never be heard unless struck.

Query:
What would strike it?

Answer:
Thought. A thought without a name
is a *sound* experience.

Soul is the feeling of Being I AM.

The Source,
until It is realized,
demands restlessness.

The Light
always includes
what is necessary for its evidence.

The point
of Self-Realization is
to be freed to acknowledge
none other than the Self,
to love none other than the Self,
and to be the Love of the Self,
and find no *other*.

Event Eight

To crack a nut
requires effort.
To enjoy the meat,
only awareness.

The fruit of nature sustains man
if he would look to see beneath the leaf.

A flower holds an opening,
a place in time
for you to take
when you blossom.

The reason the flower
isn't instantaneously in bloom
is because you put yourself
in a sequence.

The Cosmic Gardener
has given a promise
for those who would find
how to come and go at will
by stepping between the thoughts
of a Light-filled mind.

Fragrance
is that power
which is able to hold the attention
when no body is visible.[1]

As a man thinketh so will he exude. Will it be the fragrance of Being or the smell of decay?

No drug will ever give you an experience of freedom. It only gives you the semblance of what it is to experience chaos and still have a sense of being conscious.

A mystical experience is an intellectual fantasy wrapped up in the clothes of emotion, but no belt is found holding!

Most incensed natures,
when struck by the Light,
become fragrant!

The occult people
are those who are in the dark,
but tell you of its hidden glories!

A symbol of fragrance called an incense stick, when lit by the fire, is spontaneously metamorphosed, and yet the stick and its glowing head remain to hold the attention as the fragrance points to the essence of its ISness.

The symbol is the carrying agent for the experience of intuitive awareness.

When you find man and his symbols
holding you entranced,
cease viewing
from the standpoint of the symbol.

The fragrance
is always where the heart
of a full-blown experience
is present.

The garment of fragrance
moves to the current of time.
Will it go up the chimney
unappreciated,
or shall it deck your room
with anticipation?

What's a cup?
An idea for you to hold while I pour!²

The cup and saucer give one service.
Take from the cup and saucer
the fragrance,
and leave the tea.

**Man
shall never bow to man,
only in acknowledging the Beauty
undivided.**

In the Tea Ceremony you always have to bow. The
doorway is always made very small so that you have to
bow, whether you want to or not, because actually the
Presence that enables the doorway to appear is greeting
you on either side of it. It all depends upon your state of
thought whether or not you cognize it. That's the secret.

Brother Sun and Sister Moon[3]

Brother Sun and Sister Moon were all part of a canticle,
And when man could see in the Light of Love, all could
                become identical.
When a bird appeared on a rail of time and offered its
                song to Light,
The one who had a fevered brow only knew the song of
                delight.

Upon standing upright on feet so fine,
They barely touched the floor of time,
One moved in a way unto that Spot
Where the bird stood still and offered a prophecy of his
                lot.
And it took him in flight on unsteady feet
Onto the roof of the house where inspiration did keep
All thought ascending, no thought of the ground;
Don't you look down, there are falls around.

All those who gasped with such a view
Said, "Oh, he's fevered and what shall we do?"

But the birds swarmed in a net of love
And kept him from flying into their nest above.

He didn't go down to take anything out;
He just went back to the Mother of Love.
And She did take a hand of power
And brushed the cobwebs of a fevered hour.

Then in joy of a Son so fine,
Daughter moon only pined
To be embraced for only being a reflective might,
When the Son offered the glory of a powered Light.
And man said, "I will have to find
What caused the bird to sing and the poppies to shine;
What caused the butterfly to come around
When the grass was so brilliant in the Sun that's found.
I'll have to sit by the roots of a tree
and look through this grass to see the C.[4]
And then I'll go to that temple of doubt;
The walls have all crumbled but there is a Stone[5] about."

Then in the joy of meeting a love,
A man appeared and a fire of Love
Blazed upon the hearth out of time
And no intellect could encompass the Power Divine.

When man asked a question, a rock was seen.
When man asked, "What is the quest?" a temple was
                          dreamed.
When man asked for fulfillment, a song was heard,
And when man asked for cement, Love was hurled.[6]

Then in the joy of the lambkins of time,
The fruit of the ground and of the vine
Was offered as substance to the Host Unseen,
And yet acknowledged and called the Patron in deed.

This one no longer with feet of clay
Was able to engage the Enraptured Way.
And so in the glory of Love profound,
The Life that was limited to an earthly round
Bloomed as the poppies, the unseen marks of time,
And erased all the beliefs of an earthian kind;
Man awoke to a Temple so fine,
And the rock by the hearth became the One Divine.
Upon this knowing, Love stands as planned;
In the Resurrected Consciousness, Man is the Living
            Temple blessed by the Power called "I AM
            THAT I AM."

So Brother Sun took Sister Moon
And into That Day there was only High Noon.
No sun in the sky, no moon at all,
Why, the sun and the moon were One to the All.
No need of sun or moon by night
Is found in the City of pure Love's Light.

The City
is That State of Consciousness
in which nothing is
as it seems,
and is known as it IS.
When that City is known,
it can appear as the Light of His
Countenance
shining
by Its own Light.

The visionary
is one who sees visions
and translates them according to the limitations
of his thought reference.

Immaculate Sight
enables man
to fly like bird,
give prophecy's Plan.

Prophecy
to be prophecy
is the telling of That Which IS ever true
to any age that can be recorded.

The Stroke Beyond the Mind

You should take a note of meaning and find it in a book
                    of time
And say, "Ah yes, it's written, now what does this symbol
                    mean beyond the mind?"
And you know if you are to experience, you must drop
                    your thoughts and find
That the Art to the artist is not found on the artist's
                    canvas of time.
The canvas of the artist only tells a wondrous tale
That what you see on canvas points to what is Unseen and
                    which prevails —
The Power and the Glory and the Beauty and the Might
To the brush upon the canvas, and you call it one in light.

Love
is not something within you.
Love
is the unknown Somethingness
which surrounds you
and permits you to appear
as a figure of beauty,
love,
and symmetry
to anyone who is told
of Love's beauty.

A great secret of art is to know that the hand moves not, but **I** do. That's how your hand may trace a line and give a figure to a creative subject called beauty.

When art is found
the result of the Presence,
Genius is the hand.

Blueprints are usually drawings brought for observance by one who is able to capture inspiration on the nib of a pen and provide the necessary fulfillment of the demands made in the name of drawing upon the Source.

Query:
What is the definition for art?

Answer:
The action of Light to evidence beauty. When can you tell that you have produced a work of art? When you have died to being involved in the production. Now, all art is the evidence of a Principle of action appearing defined. That is the definition.

Query:
What is the ordinary person, Mr. Mills?

Answer:
An ordinary person is one who has passed through the schoolrooms of time to be educated in ignorance, and believes it true, and proves he's what he isn't by a degree!

Query:
What is dance?

Answer:
Dance is rhythm's art appearing traced.

Query:
And song, sir?

Answer:
. . is the art of sound to trace a path and man calls it melody.

Query:
What is music, Mr. Mills?

Answer:
Oh, I adore it! What is music? Music is the name given to the rapture of Being. . embraced as Love.

Query:
What is performance?

Answer:
The involuntary action of art.

Query:
Mr. Mills, what is an actor?

Answer:
The name given to one who would ape the Divine . . Action. That's an excellent question but you see, it brings a very unusual response because you have to go beyond an actor. You should have said, "What is the act?" "What is an act, Mr. Mills?" An act is the evidence of an involuntary happening appearing recognized in its impersonal power and its bestowal of grace. So therefore, an actor would have to be an impersonal partner appearing personally garbed to fulfill a graceful action on behalf of an Act of transcendent power.

The art
of communication is found
when the one communicating
is artless.

Communication
isn't getting across an idea;
communication is opening up
experience.

Is the jump in the grasshopper,
Grasshopper?
No.
It's in the act
of the grasshopper
being artless.

When the grasshopper has jumped does it scrutinize the
land it has passed over, or does it experience its nature of
"hopper?"

An artist is usually the handyman
in the service of Inspiration.

Query:
Mr. Mills, what is art?

Answer:
Being without purpose, and yet fulfilling a design.

If a line is drawn, what is the point?

If Consciousness IS, where am I?

What is the purpose of this Unfoldment? It is perhaps the ability to walk into a room where you see your Self without a mirror.[7]

Epilogue—Event Nine

*There is only
One Event,
and that is Now.*

An echo
is a recurring sound
pointing
as an arrow to the bow
from whence it sprung.

A snowflake wears translation's gown,
for in the translation,
only a tear is found.

When you have once quenched
your thirst,
water is no longer water.
It is refreshment.

You
is a suggestion that God wears
in the interlude of an earth experience.

You is nothing but a thought projection clothed in time
and space.

You
is the result
of association with division.

The belief of division
is the root of karma.[1]

Karma
is the result of an act
that doesn't bear with it
the gift of love,
respect,
and sincerity.

Karma is not what you get
for doing something wrong.
It's what you get
for not being what you are.

If you suddenly realize that the body isn't you, would you please tell me how you could be subject to a record that has to be worked out?

You cannot ascertain an accomplishment from the standpoint of a drip when you think you are apart from the ocean!

Practice enables Perfection
to appear uncontaminated
by thoughts about it.

As long as you are in the realm of comparisons, you have your world in need of resolution.

The best way to attenuate the ego is to make it accept a standard of Perfection whether it likes it or not.

The mind is given the thoughts that are commensurate with an Ideal so that it will be satisfied with a condition that is unlike it, and in this state it is willing to die and engage the Life of the Mind beyond itself.

The mind cannot grasp Truth if it is not prepared to feel its inability to see. And what can the mind see? That there is something that cannot be seen when it looks!

What the world needs now is a purified atmosphere, and I tell you, the reason it is being detected as impure is not because of the smoke stacks of industry, but because of *the needless contamination of thoughts and their forms unseen* which are contaminating your atmosphere of time. Pray the ecologists become Self-Realized for they will put an end to you and your smoke!

When the thought is freed,
what is there objective to limit?

It's your awareness
that motivates your actions;
it's your intellect that limits them.[2]

Intuition has functioned
when you suddenly realize you know
without thinking.

The ocean of Life finds you and sees you not tempest tossed, but capable of engaging the turbulence by creating a boat of consciousness, a boat, a vehicle of the Soul which can appear to ride the stormy waves of suggestion and be stilled by the knowingness that can walk on the wave and be troubled not, for in the depths of Being stillness reigns.

Consciousness
comprises the Body of Man
in the image and likeness
of Light.

Acknowledge integrity to the Self
and find what wings you shall wear!

When the bird soared on the wing,
there but for doubt go *I*.

Knowing is the answer to the question about life and
fulfills itself by wearing the name of the Quest accomplished. Knowing is the garment of praise given to the
impersonal Body of Light which enables it to happen.

When one is found
on a new line of awareness,
there is no thought
to explain.

The Infinite
is the garment of hope for the mind
until it comes to see
Limitless Nature.

Infinity,
you might say,
is the last outpost
of civilization.

Green Light

The past and the present and the future are all hung on the wheel of time. To the God Consciousness there is no past, present, or future. There isn't even the now. But Infinite Mind, ever Mindfull of its own, is able to see All. .That. .IS.

It is man who, gracefully given his share of the Kingdom as the prodigal, wanders in this world of illusion and has his past, his past lives and his past flings. Yet he knows somewhere deep within the recesses of his heart that he must return Home, and thus he sets upon a Highway, and not the byway or the bypass. It must be direct. If he is correctly motivated with sincerity, he knows that the Angel of the Lord has gone before him and thus all the lights are green.

When he returns to the Homestead, he realizes that the journey was that of a pilgrim who, with his accumulated knowledge and acquired faith, is able to relax in the realization that his meanderings have been a teaching which he brought upon himself by following the leadings other than those of his God-Being. Wearily he returns to the point of acquiescence where he says, "So help me God," and thus a condition of acceptance is opened unto him and the Angel of the Lord appears.

He realizes that all that is hung on the clock of time has brought him to the timelessness of his Divinity which has always been wound up and ready to sound forth when the wanderer relaxes in the shattering proclamation, "This is my Beloved Son in whom I am well pleased." The Son, who thought he wandered, now realizes that the understanding of his at-Onement with his spark of Divinity within is All, and that which confronts him without is nothing but the sequence of holy events strung upon that which he created as his own necessity to complete his circle upon the clock of time and return to the center and circumference of his Being. That man, no longer a wanderer but at home in his Divine Estate, walks transformed and transfigured, seeing if he wishes the play, but knowing as Christ Consciousness that he never did leave Heaven for earth.

Love is the Power
that enables you
to look at yourself,
see yourself,
and be the Self.

Notes

Event One

1
Mr. Mills comments: "The Universe is the all-enveloping Gown embracing the solar system and all that is within it, and all that is without it." He has also stated, "An organized Universe is only the compound name given to a consciousness that evidences law and order, which is to be Realized."

2
You refers to the limited personal self.

3
"Time is that lapse which seems to happen between one thought and another. And as soon as you engage the spot between two thoughts you have realized Eternity and are able to use both thoughts and unify them in an action, *now!* — K.G.M.

4
Correlative: Event Three pgs. 58-9, Five Minutes."

5
Mr. Mills has said, "I use 'I' when it can be attributed unto the Father, the Light, the Christ. And I use 'you' when you stand in the way and do not appear to know you are the Christ in the Light."

6
The "time-tunnel" is the objective time-space experience, or evolution.

7

This statement impels one to identify with those thoughts and ideas that can be attributed to an Ideal, i.e. love, sincerity, honesty, integrity, selflessness, etc., and which cannot be limited to an object in time.

8

"Experience," in this aphorism, refers to relative experience in the time-space world. Relative experience depends upon the differentiation of one object contrasted with another. When it is seen that differentiation does not necessarily imply duality, then separateness fades in the Light of One ("I is All").

9

Here it is not meant that one is to refrain from helping other people, but first to be keenly aware of how one is viewing other people who seemingly need help. According to Mr. Mills, the greatest help possible to give to another is to see him as he IS: Perfect in the Light of the Self. Then any form of outward help could naturally follow.

10

Correlative: Event Eight pg. 131, "What is the purpose of this Unfoldment? It is perhaps the ability to walk into a room where you see your Self without a mirror."

Event Two

1

Correlative: Event Nine pg. 137, "The ocean of Life finds you and sees you..."

2

The colour yellow is often the colour associated with the intellectual faculty of man and is symbolized by the sunflower in this passage — its "heart of earth" or dark centre signifying its limitations and, on another level, the unmanifested. When the intellect faces the effulgence of the Self (i.e. Sun) it realizes its own limitations and is prepared to surrender to the Infinite Power. Correlation: Event Two Pg. 44, "The mind is prepared for dying consciously..."

3

That is, consciousness cannot be found in the body. Correlative: Event Seven pg. 113, "The body proves its own purpose..."

4

Here Mr. Mills describes the timeless experience of going beyond the familiar concepts and sign-posts of the mind (i.e. "there is no *face* around").

5

Mr. Mills has given: "An Ideal is the sound given to a conscious state with the expectation of experiencing. And when experienced, who remains to have experienced the Ideal?"

6

To Mr. Mills, the attitude of searching is relative-mind orientated. It is only the person that would search for Truth because it is only the person that would identify himself as something other than Truth. When the personal approach to experience is transcended, the idea of a personal search also fades. Mr. Mills does not, however, negate the attitude of searching as a preliminary step.

7

"Images" refers to the mental symbols of experience. To think about an apple is far different than experiencing it! Correlative: Event Eight pg. 120, "When you find man and his symbols holding you entranced, cease viewing from the standpoint of the symbol."

8

Correlative: Event Four pg. 79, paragraph 1, "Thoughts are rampant..."

9

Mr. Mills has said, "The world you cannot contain in your consciousness, and yet your consciousness, limited or unlimited, constitutes your world!"

10
Mr. Mills was once asked the question, "Sir, is the world your meditation?" He answered, "The world is the cause of a suggested need to meditate!"

Event Three

1
To "leave no footprint in the sand" is to leave no "cognitive line," as the author has said. The "cognitive line" can be seen as referring to the mind's translation of experience into mental symbols, and its resultant fascination with this process. With relation to the Unfoldment, Mr. Mills has said, "The purpose of this unfolding Path is to re-awaken in man the glory of his own Essence. Thus, the Divine Self cognizing its own Allness."

2
An important discipline of the Unfoldment is to entertain and voice only those thoughts and words that magnify the Divine. To do otherwise would only bind one to the ego, referred to here as "the phantom of your drama."

3
Says Mr. Mills, "Men and women are the pictures on your screen of awareness lighted by Consciousness. If you don't have the image of the Ideal, you image after your own likeness, and what you consider yourself lacking, you tend to create in your consciousness as another."

Event Four

1
Reference is made, on one level, to the magnetic sound tape on which the Unfoldment was being recorded.

2

That is, the ability to convert a challenging experience into a learning situation.

3

Mr. Mills has stated that the impulse to attempt to unify with another person is often the unrecognized innate impetus to unify within ourselves.

4

Mr. Mills has offered: "Most people who would be practioners in the Age work from the standpoint that there is something to heal, when actually, the healing comes about through the knowingness that Essence Perfect IS."

5

"Swamp-like fragrance" refers to egotistical attitudes such as resentment, jealousy, envy, attention-getting, etc. Correlative: Event Nine, pg. 137, "What the world needs now. . ."

6

Mr. Mills comments on the idea of the leather soles never seeming to wear out: ". . . considering the idea of something Eternal through the intellectual accomplishment which always persists in trying to maintain itself."

7

Correlative: Event Nine pg. 136, "The mind is given the thoughts. . ."

8

Correlative: Event Five pg. 92, "The mind can receive only when it is empty of its thought satisfaction."

9

Quoted in an article by E.D. Dean entitled "Bridges We Cross," from the Wave Publication, March 10, 1950. On birthdays Mr. Mills has given the following: "A birthday: the record of a suggestion in the belief of an accomplishment!"

Event Five

1

One significant point here is the idea of obedience in that, in spite of not knowing the reason or "direction" of an intuitive prompting or a directive from one's Teacher, the mind must still respond like the wind.

2

To try to "finish off" thoughts only breeds more thoughts in the attempt. Mr. Mills says in Event Three, pg. 52, "You see, you'll never destroy your mind; all you do is free it from being what it isn't."

Event Six

1

"To stop your world and get off and on at will" can be correlated to the statement, "being in the world but not of it."

2

The idea of dying is symbolic in this case of something other than physical death. It represents a psychological death where one dies to the limited thoughts that one has about oneself and the world. "Dying at a slower rate of speed" signifies the prolongation of this "death" by putting it into process.

3

Mr. Mills comments: "Experiment is the hope of something new based on the ingredients of something old!"

4

Mr. Mills comments: "To initiate means to engage a stream of vital purpose, and finding the veils drop when the purpose is fulfilled — initiation!"

5

"Abstract exercises" — the metaphysical-philosophical disciplines that the student of Light engages in as part of his daily practice.

6

In this paragraph, Mr. Mills points to the fact that "Enlightenment" is a mind-term, a mental image of the Realized State. To only follow the mind's delineation of what Enlightenment is would be a kind of crucifixion in that Enlightenment would be brought into a relative framework, symbolized by the cross. Men and women are not in *need* of Enlightenment. Enlightenment IS! Says Mr. Mills, "The demand is to let the mind cease to create the conditions which it thinks surround the state of Enlightenment."

7

The door, in this case, symbolizes the threshold of a new dimension in Self-awareness.

8

To "change one's garments" refers to a limited state of awareness being dropped.

9

"Salt, water, chalk, protoplasm, or slime" refers to the physical body and its constitution.

10

"To leap" represents intuitive movement in consciousness.

11

The Phoenix is symbolic of conscious transformation and regeneration.

Event Seven

1

"Jesus was the man and Christ is the incorporeal Divine Nature. Jesus had to do with the corporeal man, and the Christ refers to the Divine Essence, and is That power which comes to the flesh to heal the belief of incarnate error as long as there is the belief of man incarnating. The Christ is that ability, the incorporeal divine ability, which enables man to come to the awareness that he is not a person incarnating, but will appear to incarnate until the belief of incarnating fades out, and then all that will be left, of course, is the Christ, the Self." — K.G.M.

2
Mr. Mills has given: "You as a body arise when your consciousness becomes dimensionalized in the three-dimensional world — limitation."

Event Eight

1
Mr. Mills has offered: "You might say that the fragrance of any flower is the unseen Soul of its power."

2
"Do you realize the teacup is only the evidence of an idea? It isn't primarily a thing. You had to have the *idea* of a teacup to recognize a teacup, and you had to have the *idea* of a me to recognize a me. And the reason you could have an idea is because you perceived what constituted a teacup or a me. Every idea has its corresponding identity, and that is not in the sentient world where matter cares for matter. The idea is lighted by the Light of Consciousness, acknowledged in the mind, and focussed as the belief of an external world. And if you really existed in an external world, I could never find you!" — K.G.M.

3
Mr. Mills gave this poem during a Sunday evening Unfoldment in response to a listener's request for his comments on the motion picture on the life of St. Francis of Assisi, "Brother Sun, Sister Moon" (Paramount Release 1973).

4
"C" refers to Christ Consciousness, the Self.

5
That is, the "Stone that the builders rejected." (Mark 12:10)

6
"Cement is the power of Love to bind." (i.e. unify) — K.G.M.

7
The mirror represents the reflective quality of mental concepts and notions.

Event Nine

1
On Karma, Mr. Mills has given the following: "Karma is the result of belief. .and man's incarnations are those flowers offered unto his coffin of belief until there is the power to restore the I to its rightful home and classification." "Karma is the belief of those who have not fulfilled a demand as far as the unification of thought and deed is concerned. In other words, it has been lip service — head minus heart!"

2
Mr. Mills has given the following definition of an intellectual: "One who is trapped by his programming and doesn't realize he's programmed!"